This edition consists of 750
Signed and numbered by the editor

Printed on Holmen Book Cream Vol 22 FSC 65 gsm
Typeset in 10.5 pt Sabon LT Std

This is number __676__

HARAULD HUGHES

Plays, Prose, Pieces, Poetry

Comprising Hughes's monumental works for the stage as well as selected poetry, lyrics, interviews, acceptance speeches, written warnings and wordless sketches, this essential volume includes extensive critical reflections by leading critics Augustus Pink, Chloë Clifton-Wright, Richard Ayoade, Leslie Francis (director of . . . *And?!*) and Hughes's final wife, Lady Virginia Lovilocke.

Plays, Prose, Pieces, Poetry brings together, for the first time, the dramas that made Hughes's name adjectival, in all-new fonts, and exhaustively punctuated according to his latest instructions.

See why some people are still calling Hughes 'the loudest play-wright of his generation'.

HARAULD HUGHES:
PLAYS
PROSE
PIECES
POETRY

Edited by Richard Ayoade

faber

First published in the UK in 2007
by Faber & Faber Ltd
The Bindery, 51 Hatton Garden
London EC1N 8HN
This new updated edition first published in 2024

Typeset by Ian Bahrami
Printed and bound in the UK by CPI Group (UK) Ltd, Croydon CR0 4YY

A CIP record for this book
is available from the British Library

ISBN 978-0-571-39308-4

MIX
Paper | Supporting
responsible forestry
FSC
www.fsc.org   FSC® C171272

Printed and bound in the UK on FSC® certified paper in line with our continuing
commitment to ethical business practices, sustainability and the environment.
For further information see faber.co.uk/environmental-policy

2 4 6 8 10 9 7 5 3 1

Contents

Introduction
by Richard Ayoade

(Note: this introduction is an edited version of a passage from *The Unfinished Harauld Hughes*, published by Faber & Faber.)

I cannot remember when someone first mentioned the name Harauld Hughes to me, but I do remember when I was first told I looked like him.

I was panning for classics in a second-hand bookshop when I looked up to see the stress-pinked eyes of the bookshop owner, Keith, a piece of white chocolate softening in his ghostly hands. 'You have a double,' he said.

This used to happen often. People would say I reminded them of someone they knew. What they tended to mean was that they had once met another person whom they couldn't confidently categorise in terms of ethnicity – a variation on 'Where are you from, *originally*?'

I said either 'Oh' or 'Huh?' or 'Right', one of those barely communicative cul-de-sacs designed to bring conversation to a close, but Keith persisted.

'Look under "H",' he said. '"H" for Hughes.'

I held up a copy of *Birthday Letters*.

'Not that windswept bastard. Harauld. H. A. R. A. U. L. D. The mother was Welsh.'

I found the name on a spine. Harauld Hughes: *The Two-Hander Trilogy*.

'Look on the back,' Keith said.

I looked. I saw the author's picture.

I had a double. Even in profile, the resemblance was remarkable. It was me.

Of course, there was a variation in age. I was sixteen and, by that stage, had written only one or two major theatrical works.

Hughes, pictured in a stark black-and-white photograph, looked to be in his thirties, had the command of a literary giant and wore the kind of glasses I would search for, in vain, from that moment on.

I opened the book and, on the inside of the dust jacket, saw the titles of the three individual plays:

Platform. Table. Shunt.

Aggressive, terse, mysterious. Within moments I was drawn into Hughes's sinister dance of suspicion and destruction.

'Would you like to read *all* of the book before you buy it?' said Keith, as he licked his upturned fingers; they were crooked, like flesh stalagmites, waxed white.

Now, with these new editions collecting a fuller picture of Hughes than we have ever had before, we can – praise be – read (nearly) all the books. Though Hughes's work is, in a sense, without end, for it lives on in the human heart. Indeed, without his work, would we even remember we *have* hearts?

Peckham, 2024

Chronology

(Note: stage plays appear in CAPITALS; films/televised plays are in *italics*.)

1931 – Harauld Hughes is born in Cardiff to Ophelia Hughes, a former missionary.

1932 – Hughes is taken to London by his 'Uncle' Clifton, known in the Elephant as 'Monkey' Perch. But Perch, dissolute, is unable to care for the boy and in any case has his own twins, Colin and Mickie, to look after. Hughes is encouraged to start primary school five years early and is looked after by various teachers.

1939 – Start of the Second World War. Hughes offers to enlist but is evacuated to Ipswich, which is its own kind of war. Went to Whepstead briefly, before running away to volunteer at RAF Martlesham. Stayed on as a junior officer, making tea and running errands.

1940 – Hughes made an honorary junior officer at the RAF base in Martlesham. He helps to develop sonar technologies by offering to fetch whatever's needed.

1945 – End of the Second World War. Hughes receives a full military discharge and moves back to London.

1946 – Hughes becomes a landlord for the first time, taking ownership of a flat near Elephant and Castle.

1954 – Hughes marries Felicity Stoat. Two years his senior, she is an established rep actress. Hughes acts under the name Monty Boat. He and Stoat have a son, Bartholomew.

1955 – Stoat cast as Boudicca in the British series *Boudicca the Brave*. Hughes cast in the supporting role of Brynlee, illegitimate brother of King Prasutagus. Leslie Francis directs some of the episodes, meeting Hughes for the first time.

1956 – Leslie Francis wins a Scottish BAFTA for his short film *Hail to Thee, O Carrot!*

1959 – Hughes's THE SITTING-DOWN DOOR (A PLAY WITHOUT WORDS) debuts at Swansea University. The student newspaper reviews it and gives it a favourable notice. The play shows 'pockets of promise'.

1960 – PLATFORM, directed by Leslie Francis, opens in the West End. The producer is Mickie Perch, though he is not involved artistically. The play receives poor notices and loses money. Harauld signs a ten-picture contract with The Anglers Production Company (which Mickie runs with his brother Colin) to offset some of the incurred loss. The accounting for this 'Recoupment' is entirely at Mickie's discretion.

1961 – TABLE opens in Guildford. It is a modest success but doesn't transfer.

1962 – ROAST and ROOST open at the Royal Court. The plays run for the rest of the year.

Hughes and Stoat move into a grand six-storey house in St John's Wood. The property is owned by Mickie Perch and rented to Hughes and Stoat in lieu of Perch's continued support for Hughes's theatrical endeavours. Perch regrets to inform Hughes that because of the high cost of the property, The Recoupment will have to be deferred until Hughes can afford to buy the property outright, which is not possible because the house is not for sale.

Hughes says he feels lost in north London and loses a stone in two weeks just by going up and down the stairs. Stoat loves the house and says she'll never leave. She never does (until she is later sectioned).

Hughes writes the poem 'Woods', though it is not about St John's Wood; 'It's about itself.'

1963 – Hughes is contracted to do uncredited script 'doctoring' on *It's a Ruddy Racket!*, directed by Leslie Francis. The film is critically acclaimed, though Hughes's (low) fee goes towards The Recoupment.

1964 – FLIGHT cements Hughes's move away from the Royal Court. Staged outside with no audience, it is not a financial success. The Recoupment starts to accrue interest. In desperation, Hughes allows Perch to pitch a TV adaptation of his theatrical works.

1965 – *The Harauld Hughes Half-Hour Play* debuts on British television. Owing to a national transport strike that leaves people stranded at home, the first episode, *Platform*, is seen by nearly half the country. The series receives wide acclaim, and Hughes becomes a publicly recognised figure. Hughes writes two new television-only plays, *Prompt* and the shorter piece *Shunt*.

1966 – *The Swinging Models*, scripted by Hughes, directed by Ibssen Anderssen and produced by Mickie Perch, is released and becomes a 'hit'. It is notable for being the first English film to feature a woman saying the word 'shit'. Despite the revenues generated, Hughes's share of the profits is negligible and entirely swallowed up by The Recoupment.

1967 – *The Especially Wayward Girl*, scripted by Hughes, is another collaboration with Anderssen and Perch. It does less well than *The Swinging Models*, but still makes a healthy profit. An 'unforeseen tax burden' means that Mickie Perch has to freeze any possibility of reducing The Recoupment for another seven years.

1968 – *The Model and the Rocker* completes *The Models Trilogy*. It is a commercial success, though a plateau, artistically.

1969 – *The Terrible Witch* is released. It starts a cycle of rip-off films, including *The Even More Terrible Witch* and *Son of a Witch*, to which Hughes contributes uncredited material. Leslie Francis's *And . . .?!* is given a special jury award at the Berlin Festival for Most Innovatively Punctuated Film.

1970 – *The Awful Woman from Space* sees Hughes explore a new milieu, 'soft SF'.

1971 – Hughes works on the screenplay for *Harlem Shuttle*, about an inner-city badminton team. The film is not made.

1972 – Hughes writes DEPENDENCE. He receives an honour for creating the Year's Longest Play in Proportion to Its Script. *The Times* describes it as 'more pause than play' and 'spectacularly hermetic'. It is his last work for the stage.

1973 – *The Deadly Gust*, Hughes's self-reflective meditation on the nature of writing. A *succès d'estime*, Ibssen Anderssen declares it to be his favourite of his collaborations with Hughes. The film loses money, leading to an increase in The Recoupment deficit.

1974 – *The Glowing Wrong*, a satirical attack on both church and state. On the penultimate day of its shoot, Ibssen Anderssen is discovered in his flat, unconscious after an overdose of antihistamines. Leslie Francis completes the last day's shooting of *The Glowing Wrong* and takes over the edit. The film is a success. Francis receives a co-directing credit.

1975 – Hughes goes through the whole year without writing, instead throwing himself into badminton. He appears in an advert for an insurance company that has the tagline: 'You handle the drama, we'll handle the insurance.' His considerable fee goes some way to offsetting The Recoupment, but he is still far from breaking even.

1976 – Hughes and Lady Virginia Lovilocke compete in a charity badminton tournament. The two become lovers.

Hughes works on the screenplay of *O Bedlam! O Bedlam!*, which is to be directed by Leslie Francis. Hughes moves out of the marital home. Lady Lovilocke tells her husband Langley that she's fallen in love with Hughes. Langley understands completely. The two men meet to discuss their good taste.

Felicity Stoat learns of the affair and begins to make a fuss. Hughes moves into Mickie Perch's Soho apartment.

Principal photography starts on *O Bedlam! O Bedlam!* Leslie Francis has a heart attack during production. Filming is halted, and the rushes are seized by the insurance company.

1977 – With the help of Langley Lovilocke, Hughes mounts a legal challenge against The Anglers' financial practices. The London offices of both Colin and Mickie Perch are raided. Hughes suffers a mini-stroke after a fight with Mickie. Hughes and Mickie part ways and will never speak again. Colin Perch attempts to drown himself in the sea but finds it too cold to go through with it. His search for a sea warm enough to contemplate death takes him to Barbados.

Ibssen Anderssen is discovered, dead, in his flat. The coroner's report rules the death to be accidental, but rumours abound of foul play.

1980 – Langley Lovilocke commits suicide, and Felicity Stoat is sectioned, leaving Hughes and Lady Virginia free to marry.

1982 – Thanks to the intervention of the Lovilocke estate, Hughes finally recoups.

1983 – Hughes writes a new poem but loses it in Belarus. Felicity Stoat commits suicide.

1986 – Hughes receives the Euripides Prize. He writes his first new piece for the theatre in nearly fifteen years, SPEECH.

1990 – The publication of *The Collected Prose and Poetry of Harauld Hughes*.

1991 – Hughes starts to write DISSIDENCE and PROVIDENCE, a seven-second diptych protesting the Gulf War. By the time he finishes writing them, in 1993, the invasion is over. The plays are staged at dawn, in the London Library, and only for non-members. The plays are then destroyed.

1997 – Hughes donates his remaining personal archive to the Elephant and Castle library. Although they weren't expecting it, they say they are happy to try and find somewhere to store it.

1998 – Hughes becomes the unofficial writer-in-residence at his local Costa Coffee.

2006 – Harauld Hughes dies.

Introduction
by Lady Virginia Lovilocke

(Note: this introduction first appeared in *The Collected Shorter Works of Harauld Hughes*, published by Faber & Faber.)

Harauld would have been thrilled by this collection of his shorter works. He was just as proud of his shorter works as he was of his longer works (though he would fiercely defend his medium-length works as well!). He would often wake me in the night to talk about politics or tell me he was cold, but frequently it would be to read to me from one of these shorter works, which he felt were especially effective when read out loudly between 3 and 4 a.m. After he had completed the recital, for which he demanded my unwavering focus, he would ask, drenched in sweat, those wonderful black eyes of his flashing, why anyone would imply that these shorter works lacked the structural integrity of the longer ones. I told him that I simply didn't understand, and that seemed to make him happy.

How fitting it is that many of these shorter works were the ones Harauld himself selected for the television programme *The Harauld Hughes Half-Hour Play*, for it was while watching *Platform*, so wonderfully staged for the broadcast by Leslie Francis, that I decided I simply had to meet the brilliant man who wrote it. We did so six years later, at a poetry recital in honour of some of the poems T. S. Eliot thought of writing, but ultimately decided not to. Harauld had a protracted physical altercation with a latecomer that ended with the man losing some of his thumb. In fact, the man's cries can be heard on the vinyl recording of the event. Fortunately, my father was a viscount, and he helped Harauld settle the matter privately. The event certainly brought Harauld and I to one another's attention, but we were both married and already in the middle of other affairs. But the pull between us was to prove irresistible.

Five years later, Harauld was competing in a charity badminton tournament to raise funds for one of those terrible conflicts that kept springing up in Africa, and asked me to join him for the mixed doubles. My children were terribly upset, of course, because they were home from school that Saturday, and after that I would be in Europe for the rest of the year, but I found myself saying yes to Harauld and, in a sense, to the rest of my life.

There were things to work out on a family level, obviously, and that was terribly difficult. I had eight or nine children, and a husband, Langley, who had always been decent, if unexciting. Harauld's then wife, Felicity Stoat, was a brilliant actress, but given to self-pity, which was very draining and one of the reasons why Harauld refused to have more than one child, a dull boy called Bartholomew, with her. Harauld and I cocooned ourselves at the Dorchester, and despite fortune's vagaries, were in a bubble of bliss from then on. But it was only after we both lost our spouses to suicide and insanity respectively that we were free to marry. Oh, joyous day!

When Harauld began to work, he would have no idea as to the length of the play that he was writing. But after a day or two, he might get a sense. 'This one's a short one,' he would say, or, 'I have a feeling this one might be long. Or longish.' Often, something he initially thought might turn out long would end up being short. These moments were especially exciting; the air around him would positively thrum with electricity. 'I thought it would be short, but it's actually quite long!' he would say, shooing a child back into the loving arms of a housekeeper.

It might have tickled Harauld, who so loved to talk, and who spent so much of his life talking to, and over, people, to find me conversing so freely in this foreword. Perhaps he knew, with these selected shorter works, that he would have the last word and that what I said wouldn't matter so very much. Harauld felt that his plays should speak for themselves, and I would agree. Indeed, these plays, though shorter than the long ones, say an awful lot, without taking up one's whole evening. Harauld loved evenings, and he loved making the most of them, without being cooped up in a theatre the whole time. 'Whatever is in me has to come out,' he would say. 'The damn length is beside the point.' How right he was, and I, for one, am pleased that these admittedly short works came out of him and are now so wonderfully reproduced in this slim volume.

I
PROSE/PIECES

Speech

*On Receiving the 1986 Euripides Prize for
Excellence in Short-Form Drama*

A long time ago, new to the craft of playwriting and even newer to the ignominies of the circus surrounding it, I was asked by a journalist – one of those pitiless limpets on civilisation's failing hull – what, exactly, my plays were 'about'. In a fit of impatience (it was my third interview of the day and I was exhausted), I replied, 'They're about the piece of grit beneath the veneer; the acid bubbling in the back of the throat; the speck of rust on the scalpel slicing into your gum.' Looking back, it's clear that I was unhappy with my dentist. But the imagery stuck and became a stick, a gritty stick, with which to beat me.

Since then, I have resisted all attempts to discuss my work. It is my deep admiration for Euripides that has brought me here tonight, forty minutes' taxi ride from an airport that is best forgotten, if not forgiven. (It was certainly not the fee, which is best described as 'honorific'.)

One of the many deprivations of my childhood was that I was denied access to the major Greek dramatists – something, ironically, for which I never forgave my mother. But, in my early teens, I discovered a slim volume of Euripides in our local bookshop after I knocked into a shelf and it literally fell at my feet. And although I had neither the money nor the inclination to buy it (the book, let alone the shop), I enjoyed seeing, and then saying, the name Euripides. I still do. 'Euripides.' I felt an immediate sense of kinship, so I bowed down to this prone tome and offered to help it back up.

In fact, I wrote a poem about it:

Euripides,
Euripides.

Get off your
Knees, Euripides.
Please. It's time
To call it a day.

A proper preoccupation of the writer is the cultivation of a good name. And, name-wise, 'Euripides' packs one hell of a wallop. It's a chicken supper with all the trimmings. For, I say to you, are we much more than our names? Have any of us gone to see an unattributed play? In terms of the theatre, there is no Chartres. A work by an unknown author is automatically a tragedy. And lest anyone mention the medieval morality plays, I'm talking about plays that people go to see *willingly*.

We go to the theatre to participate in a story about characters, yes, but we also go to participate in a story about ourselves. A story in which we are literate, sensitive and engaged. A story that places us at its centre and puts our collective big finger into the warm meat of culture's pie.

But how will *others* know just how much *we* know? For what is knowledge but a yardstick with which to beat the ignorant? How will *others* recognise *our* achievements as patrons of the arts? For what is achievement as a patron but a well-earned licence to patronise our lessers?

For this, we need names. Names with which to pepper the conversation. A conversation that isn't an actual exchange but a skirmish, a battle for dominance. A battle that is over when, through the attrition of unsolicited comment masquerading as benign observation, the other person's sense of self is fatally diminished. Only then can we rest.

To say the name Euripides or my own, Harauld Hughes, is to participate in a socially sanctioned act of cultural supremacy. And in these depraved and asinine times, we need all the ammunition we can get. I would like to thank the academy for adding my name to such an accomplished arsenal. Now you [*points to the audience*], duly sanctified, have a fresh cudgel with which to beat your neighbour. I would like to thank my long-suffering manager, Art Sparkle, for both his ruthlessness and constancy in that ruthlessness.

I would like to end there, but for contractual reasons I am prohibited from silence, even though I feel I have said all that needs to be said about the true value of drama in the public sphere.

You see, in order to accept this honour – which I felt compelled to do, both for the sake of Art (my aforementioned, still-suffering manager) and Art Itself – I have to deliver an address. There was no way out of it. I checked.

The people here tonight, Art told me, expect a speech. They have dressed up, hired a babysitter, been overcharged for buffet food and, by way of compensation, want some profundity from a visiting dignitary.

But I have always wanted my plays to speak for themselves, not I for them. Further, for me, to write a play *is* to speak. In the periods when I am unable to write because I am making love, or am too angry to make love, a sadness descends. A sadness to do with this highly temporary inability to communicate to my fellow man. Perhaps I could solve this by making love to my fellow man, but I hope I can say, without inflection, that I am simply incapable of this most ancient Greek of acts. I checked.

So, what does the playwright who refuses to speak say? Well, not very much (I hoped). My aim was to keep this as short as possible; if I am to be awarded a prize for short-form drama, ran my thinking, let this speech be an exemplar of compression. But there's brevity, and then there's taking the piss. And my original draft, said Art, the academy and, perhaps, even Art Itself, tilted towards the latter. Two minutes' stage time would not suffice, so I must suffer on.

Suffering . . . Whether it's fools or tight tendons, isn't that what we do? Isn't that what we make our protagonists do – suffer (although I do encourage them to stretch before performances)? Am I not, in this particular instance, my own protagonist? A protagonist in a drama that has been thrust upon me?

So it occurred to me that what I was writing, what I was *in*, was not, in fact, a speech, but what I always write . . . a play.

A play called *Speech*.*

The players, in sympathy with the lineage in which I find myself, are:

1. An exiled writer/philosopher; and
2. A chorus.

Enter one figure, in a mask. This is CHORUS.

CHORUS

I am Chorus. Tonight, we are but one.

THE EXILE

Aren't we all?

CHORUS

I am Chorus.

THE EXILE

You said. But since you are alone, I shall call you Solo.

CHORUS

Exile. Writer. Philosopher. Which shall I call you?

THE EXILE

Call me friend, if you can.

CHORUS

I shall call you Writer.

THE EXILE

You play the part well, Solo.

CHORUS

I play it as written, Writer.

---

* Certain Hughes scholars dispute the claim that Hughes wrote nothing substantial after 1976's aborted *O Bedlam! O Bedlam!*, citing *Speech*. Though not a full-length work, it was first performed in 1986. However, *Speech* was originally written as an introduction for *The Harauld Hughes Half-Hour Play* but was rejected on the grounds of its length. The introduction to *Speech*, though, was new (in 1986 at least) and represents the longest piece of prose that Hughes ever wrote.

THE EXILE

What news?

CHORUS

I bring news.

THE EXILE

Yes. I just asked. What is the news?

CHORUS

News is information about current events.

THE EXILE

Is that what you have brought me? A definition?

CHORUS

No. I bring news. You requested a definition.

THE EXILE

I did not request a definition. You supplied one unbidden. I know what the news is.

Chorus turns to leave.

CHORUS

Then I bid you farewell.

THE EXILE

Where are you going?

CHORUS

I came to bring the news, but you say you know what the news is, so adieu.

THE EXILE

How could I know what the news is when you haven't told me?

CHORUS

You said you knew already.

THE EXILE

That is not what I meant.

CHORUS

And yet that is what you said. Do you often say that which you do not mean?

THE EXILE

Fool.

Enter a FOOL . . .

FOOL

Yes?

THE EXILE

Not you, Fool. I was calling him fool.

FOOL

But he is Chorus. I am Fool.

CHORUS

And also, when you listed the dramatis personae, you only said you and Chorus.

The Exile turns to the Fool.

THE EXILE

Fool! You arrived unannounced.

CHORUS

You literally announced him.

THE EXILE

My characters have a habit of interrupting me.

FOOL

Who is to blame for that?

THE EXILE

I still wait for news.

FOOL

A sure way of it becoming old.

THE EXILE

Then give me the news, before it gets old.

FOOL

I have no news, only that which is old.

THE EXILE

Why do you keep thinking I'm talking to you?

FOOL

Because I'm here. And you keep talking.

CHORUS

Old news is still news.

THE EXILE

How can what's new also be old?

FOOL

For that we must ask Time.

A long pause.

Enter TIME.

TIME

I am Time.

THE EXILE

You're late.

TIME

I cannot be late. I am the indefinite progress of existence and events in the past, present and future regarded as a whole.

FOOL

In short, time waits for no man.

TIME

Nor woman.

THE EXILE

You should tell that to my wife next time I'm trying to leave the house.

FOOL

Perhaps you should ask yourself why your wife's always trying to leave the house.

THE EXILE

Perhaps you should ask yourself why you don't have a wife.

FOOL

I'd rather have a house.

THE EXILE

Then you truly are a fool.

FOOL

You haven't met my wife.

THE EXILE

You have no wife.

FOOL

That explains it.

CHORUS

There is no news.

FOOL

I've just found out I don't have a wife, and you say there's no news?

TIME

It is time. Sorry. I *am* Time.

THE EXILE

And that's time enough.

FOOL

Wait. Here comes an encore.

Enter a bearded man, wearing a toga. This is EURIPIDES.

EURIPIDES

It is I, Euripides.

Hi, Euripides.

Euripides stumbles and drops to his knees.

Euripides has fallen!

EURIPIDES

It is no tragedy to fall. Tragedy is the failure to rise again.
(*beat*)
I shall stay here a while.

ALL

Euripides,
Euripides.

(*beat*)

Get off your
Knees, Euripides.
Please. It's time
To call it a day.

Curtain.

THE SITTING-DOWN DOOR
(A PLAY WITHOUT WORDS)

Mick Barrett on *The Sitting-Down Door (A Play Without Words)* (1959)

(Mick Barrett is an actor, director and freelance chiropodist. The following is taken from Barrett's programme notes for the 1991 revival of *The Sitting-Down Door* at the Ipswich Regent.)

People forget how funny Harauld was. This play is one of his funniest, and I'm told it's also one of his most meaningful. I never asked Harauld what his plays meant. I didn't need to know. It was the first play I'd directed, so I asked his advice. He said, 'The main actor in this play is the door. Make sure you cast it right.'

The Sitting-Down Door (A Play Without Words) was first staged at the Elephant Theatre in Lambeth in 1959. The original cast was as follows:

MAN   Herbert Sand
FOOT   Patrick Rusk

Conceived and written by   Harauld Hughes
Directed by   Mick Barrett

An empty stage, save for . . .

. . . a door.

Pause.

Ding-dong.

A man appears from stage left. This is MAN.

Man approaches the door from upstage.

Opens it.

Looks through it at downstage area.

No one there.

Man exits stage left.

Pause.

Ding-dong.

Man enters stage left.

Approaches door from downstage.

Opens it.

Looks through it at upstairs area.

No one there.

Man walks stage right.

Before he reaches the right-hand side of the stage . . .

. . . the door tips forward forty-five degrees.

Man stops. Looks behind him.

Man ponders.

Then leaves.

The door falls down.

Man reappears.

Ponders.

Ding-dong.

Man ponders further.

Walks to the door. Opens it.

Looks down through the door at the stage floor.

Man looks up. Ponders.

Closes the door.

Exits towards the back of the stage.

Ding-dong.

Man stops. Looks back over his shoulder.

Walks away quickly.

DING-DONG. DING-DONG.

Man stops.

Approaches door from upstage.

Opens the door. Looks into it.

A change of expression.

A moment of apprehension.

Man attempts to shut the door.

*A FOOT – chalk white, clad in a half-broken boot – emerges
from beyond the doorframe and resists Man's attempt to close it.*

A struggle.

Man prevails.

The door is closed.

Man looks up.

The Foot kicks the door open. Again, Man pushes the door closed, forcing the Foot down.

Now Man sits on the door.

We hear a periodic thump against the door.

Thump. THUMP. Thump.

Slow fade.

II
PLAYS

PLATFORM

Introduction
by Augustus Pink

(Note: this introduction first appeared in *The Collected Harauld Hughes Half-Hour Plays*, published by Faber & Faber.)

Plays don't work on television. Or so the received wisdom went. The intimacy and presence of theatre could not be replicated on the small screen. The actors, overlit to accommodate the needs of the primitive multi-camera format, looked hot and uncomfortable, declaiming to an unseen audience who were, via the miracle of the lens, closer to them than their theatre-going counterparts could ever be. The whole endeavour had an air of overcooked falsity.

Until Harauld Hughes. How often have we had to say that?

It was 1965. Skirts were getting shorter, labour was cheap and Irish, racism could still be casual, and we all agreed that there *was* a correct way to speak (with a special exception for The Beatles, because they were such fun). A national railway strike, which left many unable to get to the office, coupled with a signalling fault on Britain's other television channel meant that Hughes's first televised play, *Platform*, had a captive audience of close to fourteen million people. The piece, a commercial disaster when it was put on at the Royal Court, suddenly became a smash. No doubt this had something to do with Donny Chapel (nicknamed 'The Teeth' by his army of teenage fans) playing the key role of Rocker*

---

* The figure of the rocker is a resonant one for Hughes. There are rock 'n' roll figures in each of his first three films – *The Swinging Models*, *The Especially Wayward Girl* and *The Model and the Rocker*. But in later films the lone rocker, perhaps influenced by the rise of beat music, becomes part of a band. This new corporate being seems to cause Hughes's interest to wane. There is a lobby band in *The Terrible Witch*, but they are barely featured. And in *The Awful Woman from Space*, an entire group dies in a road accident. A literal and figurative death?

(note: the definite article is deliberately withheld from the character's name, a typically Hughesian touch). But while these teenyboppers may have persuaded their parents to tune in, it was the parents who became turned on (nine months later, there was a spike in the birth rate) and continued to turn up for subsequent broadcasts.

Hughes's plays, with their arrhythmic cadences and charged, liminal settings anchored in the domestic, connected to people in a way that bewildered the critics. His was a new type of writing. Tough. Tender. Unsparing. Lean. What would be confusing in a pork chop made perfect sense in the world of Harauld Hughes.

And then there was Hughes himself – polo neck, thick sideburns, black glasses – playfully introducing the works in his commanding baritone and with his seductive mastery of language, reminding us that he was an actor himself.

I interviewed Hughes several times throughout his career. He was a tough man to pin down, whether in conversation or on a judo mat. He detested journalists with a passion I've rarely seen. He simply couldn't understand why anyone would think they could find out what someone else thought by asking questions. Hughes didn't mind questions per se; indeed, he would fire them at me with alarming rapidity ('What are you doing here?' 'What on earth were you thinking?' 'Are you trying to be stupid?'), but he never expected a response. The answer, he seemed to be saying, was already in the question.

Perhaps Hughes's most 'realistic' play, *Platform* artfully interrogates who we are trying to be, and for whom, and for how long, and also why, and when. This dissection of class, gender and skiffle is as powerful now as it was then.

Platform was first performed upstairs at the New Lyric in 1960, before moving downstairs. During the transfer, it became lodged between floors. New seating was arranged until the original cast could be cut free and returned to rep. They were:

ACTRESS	Felicity Stoat
ROCKER	Mick Barrett

The television adaptation for *The Harauld Hughes Half-Hour Play* (1965) was faithful to the original, with the addition of Hughes's introduction and a new prologue, which was filmed on location. It featured the following cast:

ACTRESS	Inger Marie
ROCKER	Donny Chapel
HARAULD HUGHES	Himself
GOD	Edmund Butterby
MANDY	Felicity Stoat

Both the original theatre production and the TV broadcast were directed by Leslie Francis.

INT. STAGE

A bare stage.

HARAULD HUGHES is dressed in black.

He finds the light. The faint, sensual suggestion of sweat on his brow.

He addresses us in his unhesitating, sonorous voice.

> HARAULD
> My name is Harauld Hughes. I write plays. I don't know what they mean, any more than I know what God meant when He created the world.

Enter GOD. White beard. Robes. The usual.

> GOD
> I am God. My reasons are my own.

> HARAULD
> God doesn't explain Himself.

> GOD
> So why should Harauld?

> HARAULD
> We are not, by nature, given to transparency.

> GOD
> Though people often mistake Me for a gas.

> HARAULD
> People make mistakes.

> GOD
> I am not *not* a gas. But that is not the same as *being* a gas.

HARAULD

Another thing that God and I have in common is that we both work fast.

GOD

If I can fashion the universe in six days . . .

HARAULD

Says God, in that provocative tone of His . . .

GOD

. . . how long can it take to write a play?

HARAULD

Perhaps it is more difficult to write a play than it is to make the world.

GOD

Perhaps.

Silence.

But roughly . . . How long? For a play?

HARAULD

A play should come out in one go. Like a tooth.

A pause.

GOD

It feels like there should be more to it than that.

HARAULD

Well, there isn't.

A broiling, darkening sky appears behind God. A violent wind. Leaves swirl. God's eyes glow white.

Harauld is unmoved.

GOD

Fine. You win.

(*beat*)

Can I go now?

HARAULD

It's Your world, I just live in it.

GOD

Okay then. Bye.

God glows red and then disappears into a cloud of mist.

The mist blows towards Harauld and engulfs him.

The lens, too, is overtaken by the mist. When it clears, Harauld is in a cobbled street.

He walks up a hill and sees ROCKER on the other side of the street, carrying a guitar.

The two men exchange glances.

HARAULD
(V.O.)

But, like my Mysterious Friend, I never work on Sundays. Sundays are for masculine activities – badminton, love-making and pub lunches. But that doesn't stop me setting a play on a Sunday. A Sunday evening, to be precise, in the drizzle of England's deprived north.

FADE TO:

EXT. STREETS – NIGHT

A high-angled shot over a small town. Harauld walks one way, Rocker the other.

Our title fades up: 'PLATFORM'.

INT. MAKE-UP TRUCK – NIGHT

A figure with a hot towel to her face. Steam rises from it.

A pair of tongs enters the frame to take the towel.

The figure senses that it's time to give the towel back.

We reveal an ACTRESS (40). She looks at herself in the mirror.

She thanks the owner of the tongs.

We hear a voice off. The Actress turns round to see MANDY (40s), her make-up artist.

> MANDY
> Are you sure you don't want a lift?

> ACTRESS
> I'll just walk. It's not too far.

> MANDY
> It's raining a bit.

> ACTRESS
> That's fine.

> MANDY
> Sure?

> ACTRESS
> I've stuck my head out the door and it's barely a drizzle.

> MANDY
> Well, you're braver than me.

> ACTRESS
> I doubt that.

CUT TO:

EXT. STREETS – NIGHT

The Actress runs through the rain. It's particularly heavy. She has pulled her light summer coat up over her head.

In her other hand, a suitcase, tightly gripped.

We recognise the street from earlier.

CUT TO:

EXT. RAILWAY PLATFORM – NIGHT

An isolated railway station somewhere in the north of England.

*Thoroughly sodden, the Actress walks to the noticeboard.
It indicates that the train to London is about to leave in one
minute. She checks the platform number.*

She is not on the right platform.

*She tries to calculate whether she will be able to get to the other
platform in time.*

*She decides to try, but before she even gets to the stairs to cross
the platform, the train starts to pull away.*

She looks back at the board. The next train is not for an hour.

*We see her from the other side of the platform, looking small
and lonely against a dark sky. A shoulder enters the frame.*

*We see the Actress's perspective: a man, dressed in black,
holding a guitar.*

CUT TO:

INT. WAITING ROOM – NIGHT

The Actress walks into a waiting room.

*A man sits in a seat in the corner, leaning up against a guitar
case. He is slightly younger than the Actress.*

*He is the man we saw earlier: a Rocker. He wears black
jeans, boots and a jean jacket. He is in marked contrast to the
ostensibly more 'grown-up', neat Actress . . .*

*The Actress takes off her coat, shakes off as much rain as she
can and places it over the back of a chair.*

*She looks at the drinks machine and searches in her bag for a
few coins.*

ROCKER

It's broken.

ACTRESS

The machine?

ROCKER

No. Britain.

(*beat*)

Of course the machine.

ACTRESS

There's no need to be so rude.

ROCKER

I know. I'm rude purely for my own enjoyment.

He reaches into his coat pocket for his pack of cigarettes.

Cigarette?

ACTRESS

I don't smoke.

ROCKER

You're one of those health nuts.

ACTRESS

I don't like the smell.

ROCKER

Neither do I. I just prefer it to the smell of everything else.

(*beat*)

Cant, mainly.

He lights his cigarette.

C–A–N–T.

ACTRESS

Thank you. I know how to spell.

ROCKER

(*ignoring her*)

Give or take a letter.

*His hair is swept up into a rockabilly pompadour. He takes out
a comb and runs it through his mop.*

So, you like to talk, I see . . .

ACTRESS

It depends on the company.

ROCKER

And what, if I may ask, is the kind of company you like to
keep?

The Actress turns.

ACTRESS

Look, I'm very tired, I've had a long day, I just want to
rest.

ROCKER

I'd be careful about resting on your laurels, though. You've
already missed one train. The next one's the last.

ACTRESS

Your concern is touching.

ROCKER

I'm a very considerate fellow.

The Actress snorts.

You may scoff or, indeed, snort, but if you fall asleep,
which even the best of your kind has been known to do,
you risk a night of fatal exile, floundering in the feral
north.

The Actress sits down. She closes her eyes.

Will hubby be waiting up?

ACTRESS

How should I know?

ROCKER

Still punishing you, is he?

ACTRESS

What on earth are you talking about?

ROCKER

In my experience, if you don't conform – by which I mean, if you're expected to do certain things, and then don't do those certain things – censure, verbal or other, will soon follow.

ACTRESS

My husband does not punish.

ROCKER

I'm not talking about anything so crude as a smack. You're both far too bourgeois for such proletarian cruelties. I'm talking about the very many ways in which people can make their feelings known, and the destruction that can ensue therefrom.

The Actress looks at him for some time. Then . . .

ACTRESS

Am I making my feelings known?

ROCKER

You, if I may say so, are doing everything in your power to *stop* your feelings from being known.

ACTRESS

If you had any perception whatsoever, my feelings towards you would be quite clear.

ROCKER

They are. And I'm very flattered.

ACTRESS

I think you might be the most conceited man I've ever met.

ROCKER

So you do agree we've met? We have become acquainted?

ACTRESS

We're on the same platform.

ROCKER

And even though there are two platforms to choose from, we've ended up on the same one.

ACTRESS

I didn't come over here to be with you. I came over here because this is where my train leaves from.

ROCKER

Freud would say there are no accidents.

ACTRESS

Are you saying I missed my train deliberately?

ROCKER

I'm saying old Sigmund might have drawn a conclusion or two from your conspicuous dawdling.

ACTRESS

I was checking the timetable. I was looking for the right platform.

ROCKER

In a manner that might strike the father of psychoanalysis as somewhat leisurely. 'She's not going to catch the train to London if she carries on in that leisurely fashion,' he would have said, as he puffed on a phallic symbol.

ACTRESS

You saw me?

ROCKER

I think that is no longer a secret.

ACTRESS

You knew I was trying to catch the London train?

ROCKER

It seemed a fair enough assumption for your humble narrator to make.

ACTRESS

And yet you didn't see fit to call out and tell me I was about to miss it?

ROCKER

I didn't know you then.

ACTRESS

You don't know me now!

ROCKER

I have nothing against helping out a friend. Even an acquaintance. But a stranger . . . I wouldn't have the nerve.

ACTRESS

You're all nerve.

ROCKER

Spoken like a true dentist.

ACTRESS

I'm an actress.

ROCKER

That's what all the dentists say.

ACTRESS

Don't you believe I'm an actress?

ROCKER

See! A real question, ladies and gentlemen, our first of the evening. It's not too hard, is it?

ACTRESS

That's not the first question I've asked.

ROCKER

I said the first 'real' question. 'How do we know it's a real question?' asks the attendant multitude. Because you care about the answer. All your previous questions were just to fob me off or catch me out, but you actually care about whether you come across as an actress.

ACTRESS

And why's that?

Rocker pauses.

ROCKER

Because you're impossibly vain. For good reason.

ACTRESS

Is that a tactic of yours? Cruelty with sugar sprinkled on top?

ROCKER

It seems like you've answered your own question.

ACTRESS

I have another: what are *you* waiting for?

For the first time, Rocker hesitates.

Don't worry about it – I actually don't care.

ROCKER

It seems that you start with the sugar.
(*beat*)
I am waiting for the London train.

The Actress thinks.

ACTRESS

When I arrived, the train to London hadn't as yet left.

ROCKER

That is the order of events, as far as I am aware, m'lud.

ACTRESS

But you were on the correct platform?

ROCKER

Let the record state I was.

ACTRESS

So you could have got the train?

ROCKER

Let the record state that the smouldering man with the guitar *could* have caught the train.

ACTRESS

So why didn't you?

ROCKER

I thought I might enjoy meeting you.

ACTRESS

I see.

ROCKER

Can't always be right.

ACTRESS

No one forced you.

ROCKER

Well, I thought you might be a dentist. And I've always liked dentists.

ACTRESS

You *deliberately* missed the train.

ROCKER

You see, that's where I disagree. I didn't choose to not get that train. I was compelled.

ACTRESS

Compelled? By whom? An unseen hand? God?

ROCKER

I don't think we can blame Him or His see-through mitts on this occasion.

ACTRESS

So who can we blame?

ROCKER

This empty, cruel world.

ACTRESS

Yes, I rather took you for a nihilist.

ROCKER

Then, madam, you mistook me.

ACTRESS

So you believe in God?

ROCKER

Oh, no. I'm Church of England.

The Actress gives a quick dismissive look.

I find the Church of England to be less ethically prescriptive. Nihilism requires such a committed rejection of absolutes that if you're not careful, you can find yourself believing in something, and then – wallop – you're out of the club. You hear of lapsed Catholics, but no one lapses from the Church of England. From what would one be lapsing? Half a millennium of well-meaning vagueness? No one's been chucked out of the Church of England for a mere trifle like losing their faith. Out of interest, what brings you north of the Home Counties?

ACTRESS

I told you. I'm an actress.

ROCKER

And is there no work down south? I was worried this day would come. London theatres boarded up after the great dramatic purge. Hordes of thespians out on their finely attuned ears, forced to declaim in the street and so forth . . .?

ACTRESS

I'm making a film.

ROCKER

And how does hubby feel about you coming up north, taking work away from hard-working locals?

ACTRESS

He says he's happy as long as I am happy.

ROCKER

One of those relativists, eh? You want to be careful. Because if he's happy as long as you're happy, he'll also be sad as long as you're sad. And, from the look of you, you've been sad for a little while now.

ACTRESS

It always astonishes me that people don't think they are
part of why someone looks the way they do. As if they can
be neutral observers whose presence in no way affects the
mood of the person they're with. Perhaps you have a role
to play in my looking sad.

ROCKER

I'd say I have the starring one.

ACTRESS

Don't build up your part.

ROCKER

I'm very happy with my part as it is. What part does your
husband play?

ACTRESS

He doesn't like to act.

ROCKER

He's not part of the company?

ACTRESS

He has his own.

ROCKER

I bet he does. There are few greater thrills than finance.

ACTRESS

He's actually in shipping.

ROCKER

Really? When does he arrive?
                    (beat)
Where did you meet?

ACTRESS

At a play.

ROCKER

One of his?

ACTRESS

One of mine.

ROCKER

I didn't know they staged plays at the docks.
(*beat*)
What's his favourite kind of cargo container?

ACTRESS

I don't know.

ROCKER

Secretive fellow?

ACTRESS

He keeps no secrets.

ROCKER

Not that you know of.

ACTRESS

You should be careful whom you accuse.

ROCKER

And you should be careful whom you marry.

ACTRESS

I was. I am.

ROCKER

Don't forget the future tense.

ACTRESS

I will not be marrying again.

ROCKER

Probably for the best. Stay single.

ACTRESS

I'm married!

ROCKER

But for how long?

ACTRESS

Do you play in a group?

ROCKER

Yes. The string section went on ahead.

ACTRESS

You're a guitarist.

ROCKER

I just like the case. I'm actually a singer.

ACTRESS

What do you sing?

ROCKER

The wrong notes, mainly.

(*beat*)

All you needed to say was that you loved him. But you never did.

ACTRESS

Is that one of your numbers?

ROCKER

You know what I mean.

ACTRESS

Why would I tell you what I mean?

ROCKER

Because I'm part of the world. And when you're in love, that's who you tell.

ACTRESS

You're not part of any world I want to be part of.

ROCKER

Is that why you've come all the way up here? To be in a pretend one?

ACTRESS

Are your songs not pretend?

                              ROCKER
My songs are very real.

                              ACTRESS
And so is this film.

                              ROCKER
What's the film about?

                              ACTRESS
I don't want to spoil it for you.

                              ROCKER
I have a feeling that won't be possible.
                              (*beat*)
Please.

                              ACTRESS
How much do you want to know?

Rocker indicates with a 'the fish was this big' gesture . . .

                              ROCKER
This much.

                              ACTRESS
Seems like you can take it or leave it.

                              ROCKER
Fine, then.

He gestures a bigger fish.

This much.

                              ACTRESS
I'd throw that one back.

                              ROCKER
You need to take into account the load-bearing capacity of
my rod.

The Actress will not rise to the bait.

ROCKER

I don't know what the deviants in shipping get off on, but I'm no masochist.

ACTRESS

. . .

ROCKER

Fine.

He gets down on his knees.

ACTRESS

What are you doing?

ROCKER

What does it look like? I'm on my knees.

ACTRESS

That is no concern of mine.

Rocker looks confused. He stands up, walks over to the edge of the platform and . . .

. . . jumps.

He is now on the track.

The Actress runs over.

What do you think you're doing?

ROCKER

I'm waiting for the London train.

ACTRESS

You're obstructing the line.

ROCKER

Who are you – signal control?

ACTRESS

Come on. Enough's enough.

ROCKER

I like it down here. In fact, I might lie down, like damsels
of old, when tied to the tracks.

He lies down.

You should try it one day. You can feel the vibrations.

ACTRESS

It's a film about a young man who wants to leave a small
town.

ROCKER

What's stopping him?

ACTRESS

His parents. The education system. Inertia.

ROCKER

His own wayward legs!

ACTRESS

And he spends the day thinking up these little stories.
Sketches, really. And the film shows these flights of fancy as
we go along.

ROCKER

Sounds like a wonderfully inventive way to physicalise his
interior world.

ACTRESS

But what he really wants is his own show on TV – it'd be
a show about his life in a boring town and his flights of
fancy.

ROCKER

Where does he get his ideas?

ACTRESS

And he's always running after girls . . .

ROCKER

They go very fast, those girls.

ACTRESS

Which gets him into trouble.

ROCKER

The course of true running ne'er went smooth.

ACTRESS

So he writes a script and sends it to the BBC, to me – I play
a TV executive – and my character reads it and thinks it's
wonderful, and we invite him to London and say, would he
be prepared to do a little screen test? But he's late. And hung-
over. And unprepared. So my boss tells him where to go.

ROCKER

Very kind of him to give him directions after all that.

ACTRESS

But I think he has potential, so I come up on the train to
try to convince him to try again, and we end up having an
affair.

ROCKER

Is she married?

ACTRESS

Yes.

ROCKER

How does it end?

ACTRESS

If you come up onto the platform, I'll tell you.

Rocker remains on the tracks.

ROCKER

Does her husband know about this brilliant young man?

We start to hear the low rumble of a train approaching.

ACTRESS

The train's coming.

ROCKER

That's not an answer.

The Actress is starting to sound panicked.

> ACTRESS
>
> No, he doesn't. The husband doesn't know.

> ROCKER
>
> Is she planning to tell?

> ACTRESS
>
> I don't know. I mean, it's not in the script.

The sound of the train gets closer. Lights come up.

> ROCKER
>
> And what's not in the script doesn't happen?

> ACTRESS
>
> I suppose. Oh, please will you get off the tracks?

> ROCKER
>
> What's it to you? I'm the most conceited man you've ever met. My songs aren't even real. Good riddance, I'd say.

> ACTRESS
>
> I didn't mean it.

> ROCKER
>
> You should be careful with your words. Especially in your profession.

> ACTRESS
>
> Just come back to the platform.

> ROCKER
>
> Why?

> ACTRESS
>
> This isn't fair. This is a silly stunt.

> ROCKER
>
> What did you call me?

> ACTRESS
>
> Stop it! I can't take it! Please! I can't watch you killing yourself.

ROCKER

I can't watch you slowly die!

The Actress puts her hands over her eyes. The noise is getting quite loud now.

Rocker stands up.

I'll step onto the platform if you answer one question: do you love your husband?

Our camera moves close, into a close-up, over the course of which the lights from the train grow dazzlingly bright.

ACTRESS

No! I hate him. I hate his boring voice and his whistly breath and his ratty teeth and his smell and his inwardness and his vaporous gaze that never takes me in or cares for me or notices me or shows any interest but just consumes and obliterates and kills me. He's killing me. He's killed me. He's made me die.

The sound of the train reaches its full pitch. She jumps.

We cut wide. We see both Rocker and the Actress standing on the tracks. Behind them is a train.

The Rocker indicates towards it.

ROCKER

That's the London train.

The Actress opens her eyes and looks around. She smiles.

This station is a terminus. At a certain point the trains come in, stop and go back the way they came. Or, to put it in other words, we're on the wrong platform.

ACTRESS

That's where you're wrong. I think, for the first time in my life, I'm on the right one.

They look at one another.

ROCKER

If we run, we could still make it.

ACTRESS

Why would we run?

We hold.

Cut to black.

TABLE

Introduction
by Augustus Pink

The early works of Hughes are characterised by a yearning to communicate. Though the milieux of *Platform* and *Table* couldn't be more different – one set in the north of England, one in the south – both concern a Man, a Woman and a Misunderstanding. Is there an older story? And yet Hughes makes it new. In *Platform*, a man takes on the role of inquisitor. This 'Rocker' (as he is known, for he has no other given name) represents a new kind of Englishman, acerbic, witty, irreverent and counter-cultural. This is the revolution to come. In *Table*, it is the woman ('She') who questions the prevailing male orthodoxy, with devastating results.

Conceived as another two-hander, *Table* shows Hughes moving away from the proletarian domain of his earlier work and turning his attention on the not-so-discreet bourgeoisie. Though from a modest background (one of his parents was Welsh), Hughes soon found himself among the London literati, with their 'wooden salad bowls, winter sun and flat-weave rugs'. He was fascinated by the fact that there was an entire class of people who, unbidden, would tell you where they got their furniture from or what they hoped to do with their lofts; men who thought knowing a great deal about wine was a sufficient substitute for having a personality, and that wearing jeans on the weekend made them look relaxed. But Harauld refused to judge, and before long he found himself looking for the perfect farmhouse table for his new Georgian house in St John's Wood and using the word 'supper' without self-consciousness.

The character of Sebastian (incarnated, definitively in my view, by Edmund Butterby) was added in a later draft. Much has been written about what Sebastian is doing under the table, but Hughes never answers the question, nor gives any indication as to how Sebastian got there. Butterby came to resent the part, saying,

'There's more to me than some bloke under a table.' So, in *The Harauld Hughes Half-Hour Play* version, Sebastian is played by Hughes himself, which gives the character an extra resonance. Hughes, the writer, puppets from below.

Table was first performed al fresco in the round in 1961, then in a square, and finally in a roaming rhomboid with an alternating pivot point. It then moved inside and had a brief run at the Old Almeida, before being transferred back into rehearsals. The original cast was as follows:

SHE	Felicity Stoat
HE	Mick Barrett
SEBASTIAN	Edmund Butterby

In the television adaptation the cast was as follows:

SHE	Inger Marie
HE	Herbert Sand
SEBASTIAN	Harauld Hughes
HARAULD HUGHES	Himself
A SWELLING	Felicity Stoat
DOCTOR	Dinki Gustavsson

INT. STAGE

A bare stage.

HARAULD HUGHES is dressed in black.

He finds the light . . .

. . . and addresses us.

> HARAULD
>
> My name is Harauld Hughes. I write plays because I have
> to. I don't want to; they pour out of me. And unless I allow
> myself to excrete, the consequences can be lethal. Once, I
> stopped writing for a month because I was having an affair
> with a beautiful economist, and so much dramatic tension
> built up inside me that I developed a swelling below my
> right sideburn.

Enter an actor. Red, hairy, bad teeth.

> A SWELLING
>
> I am A Swelling.

CUT TO:

*Harauld starts to walk along a corridor. The Swelling follows
him.*

> HARAULD
>
> I tried to ignore it, but it grew so large I was worried I'd
> have to widen the doors in my already-substantial house.

*Harauld and the Swelling race towards a door at the end. They
can't both get through.*

A struggle/fight ensues on the floor.

CUT TO:

INT. SURGERY – DAY

Harauld sits uncomfortably close to his Swelling.

A DOCTOR enters our frame.

> HARAULD
> (V.O.)
> I went to visit my beautiful doctor.

Indeed she is.

She raises a crossbow and aims at the Swelling.

A close shot of an arrow speeding through the air.

Close shot of the Swelling, the arrow through its throat.
The Swelling runs around, screaming. We alternate between
the reactions of Harauld and the Doctor as they look at the
Swelling, which shrinks down to a puddle of pus and blood on
the chequerboard floor.

The Doctor and Harauld crouch down and look at the depleted
Swelling.

The Doctor steps on the remains with her shoe.

> HARAULD
> (V.O.)
> Pus, blood and a new two-hander leaked out of me.

The Doctor looks at Harauld, her eyes filled with desire.

Two medical orderlies bring in a screen just as they embrace. We
see their outlines in silhouette.

The curtain is removed and, via an invisible wipe, we find
ourselves back on the stage.

Harauld is under a single spotlight.

HARAULD

A two-hander called *Table*. I cannot tell you anything
about it, except that I think I wrote it. But I can tell you
something as to the circumstances of its conception. I
walked into a room and saw a table. Next thing I knew, I
had a play. Now we give it to you.

He looks upstage.

The lights on him fade, and we bring them up on . . .

CUT TO:

INT. ROOM – MORNING

*We hold on an empty room. Is it a set or is it a real room? It is
hard to tell.*

*It has the feel of a room that has been abandoned. Dusty. Walls
a little scuffed.*

A caption: 'TABLE'.

A door in the background swings open.

The caption disappears.

A woman and a man walk through the door.

SHE

What's this?

HE

It's whatever we want it to be.

SHE

It's hardly that.

HE

You know what I mean.

63

SHE

I don't. I really don't know what you mean.

HE

It's another room. That's what it is.

SHE

Ah. A room. It's a room.

HE

Don't start.

SHE

Oh, I haven't.

HE

Haven't what?

SHE

Started.

There is a pause.

What was it?

HE

The room?

SHE

What else?

HE

I think it was the dining room.

SHE

It's rather small for a dining room.

HE

Well, that's London.

SHE

What is?

HE

London.

                            (*beat*)
London's London.

                    SHE
And that's that.

                    HE
Well, yes.

                    SHE
'Come to London: it's too small for a dining room.'

                    HE
You know what I mean.

                    SHE
You keep saying that. But I don't know what you mean. I
simply haven't the slightest idea what you mean.

                    HE
I mean, this was a dining room.

                    SHE
It's barely big enough for a table.

                    HE
Depends on the table.

                    SHE
Well, I was thinking of one of those tables that you could
sit around. Perhaps with others. One that would be big
enough to accommodate plates. And perhaps the odd glass.
That kind of table.

                    HE
Come off it. You can fit a table in here. Easy.

                    SHE
I think a house should be a place that can contain people.

                    HE
What are we?

                    SHE
Less than that.

(*beat*)

And it's not 'easy'. 'Easy' is the last thing this is.

A pause.

I used to know so many people that they couldn't fit in this room.

HE

Well, let's not allow a table to displace those memories of better times.

SHE

I didn't say they were better. Why are you lying about what I said?

HE

I didn't say you said they were better.

SHE

Yes, you did. Or at least you implied it.

HE

It was you who implied those times were better. I merely picked up on the implication.

SHE

What implication?

HE

The implication of the times.

SHE

Which times?

HE

Those times. The times. You know. Before.

SHE

Ah! Before. I remember it well.
(*beat*)
Yes, before was better.
(*beat*)
Not that now takes much beating.

HE

Do you want to see if it'll fit?

SHE

What's 'it'? What's this 'it' you're trying to fit?

HE

The table.

SHE

Which table are you talking about? The tiny one of your
imagining?

HE

No. The table. The actual table. Your table.

SHE

It's not my table.

HE

Then whose table is it?

SHE

It's never been my table.

HE

Then what have we been doing with it all these years?

SHE

I was looking after it.

HE

In loco parentis mensae?

SHE

When you speak, do the words come straight out or do
they come via some kind of thought? I mean, I know
you have thoughts to do with yourself. I often hear them
in monologue form. Obsessively buffed with self-pity's
dull cloth. Honed by years of repetition. But I'm talking
– with an optimism that would be almost touching were
it not so tragically misplaced – about the possibility of
what *I* say having some kind of bearing or effect on what

you say. I suppose you could even go as far as to call it a conversation. Not just hitting the ball over the net.

A pause.

HE

I was asking if you wanted to see if the table would fit. In real life. In this room. That was all. There is no ball. There is no net. There's just this table. This blasted table.

SHE

Nothing else?

HE

No.

SHE

Because I feel that's not all you were asking.

HE

Well, I can't speak to your feelings.

SHE

To what are you speaking, if not my feelings?

A pause.

HE

I'm an orphan too.

SHE

I suppose that makes me Orphan One.

HE

I don't think we should live our lives around a table.

SHE

Yes, but do you want us to live at all?

HE

It's just a table.

SHE

Nothing is just a table.

HE

Not even a table?

SHE

Especially not a table. Especially not that table.

HE

For me, a table is a table.

SHE

A table is a table.

HE

As far as I'm concerned.

SHE

And how far are you concerned? How far does your concern extend?

HE

Far enough.

SHE

But not too far. There is no room for excess. Your leaves hang limp.

HE

Is your concern unbounded?

SHE

A table is a table. A room is a room. London is London. You're a poet of tautology. What's your next collection called? *It Is What It Is*?

HE

What's it to you?

SHE

The table?

HE

What else?

A pause.

SHE

And if the table doesn't fit, then what?

HE

Then it doesn't fit.

SHE

That's right. But then what?

HE

Well, then it doesn't fit.

SHE

That, I feel, has been established. My question, and wish
me luck, studio, is: then what?

HE

I don't know what you mean.

SHE

Would you like to find out?

A *pause.*

HE

How would I find out?

SHE

Is that a genuine question?

HE

What else would it be?

SHE

Ooh, I don't know. An insincere one?

HE

Either answer it or don't answer.

SHE

That's rather binary, even for you.

HE

What's that meant to mean?

SHE

You seem to be on a perennial search for meaning. Perhaps you were hoping to find it in this room.

HE

No luck so far.

SHE

Perhaps you haven't gone far enough.

HE

What happens if it doesn't fit?

A pause.

If the table doesn't fit, what do we do?

SHE

That's the question, isn't it? What do we do?

HE

Look, aren't we jumping the gun a bit? Shouldn't we at least see?

SHE

See?

HE

Yes. I think we should at least do that.

SHE

Before we think, we should see. Our poet turns empiricist.

HE

I don't think wanting to find out whether the table fits makes me Jeremy bloody Bentham.

SHE

His middle name was Sebastian. And he was a utilitarian.

HE

My name is Jeremy Bentham, and I'm a utilitarian. It's been five years since I've regarded utility as the sole measure of something's value.

SHE

'It is the greatest happiness of the greatest number that is the measure of right and wrong.'

HE

And how does that work when there are only two of you?

SHE

It rather suggests that there should be more than just two of you. Otherwise you've not really formed the basis for a thriving society.

HE

Who would you like to join us?

SHE

In this room? Someone small.

A pause.

I lied to you earlier.

HE

About being happier before?

SHE

No. That's true. I was happier before. I lied about Jeremy Bentham.

HE

About his being a utilitarian?

SHE

About his having a middle name.

HE

I'll never forgive you.

SHE

Did you know he was a prodigy? Studying Latin by the age of three. By seven he would play Handel sonatas for dinner guests.

HE

I can see why he didn't have time for a middle name. It's a shame he's no longer with us. He could have serenaded us from under the table.

SHE

When was he with you? Who is with us? Who is with you?

HE

Who is with me?

SHE

Who is with you?

HE

You, for a start.

SHE

I'm just for the start, am I? Who is to follow? Who would you like at your table? Or under your table?

HE

Not on the table?

SHE

Don't be vulgar.

A pause.

HE

He was called Sebastian, wasn't he?

SHE

Still is, as far as I'm aware.

HE

So, in a way, you didn't lie when you said Sebastian.

A pause.

But it's not his middle name. It's ours. It's a name in the middle of us. A name on the table. A name in the table.

SHE

It wasn't what you thought.

HE

I thought it was something more than a thought. But perhaps I'm being empirical again. I never would have thought of that. Not on a table. Not with his frame. How did it hold?

SHE

How did it hold?

HE

Yes. How did it hold?

SHE

How did what hold?

SHE

The table.

SHE

It's a substantial table.

HE

He's a substantial man. For someone who lacks all substance.

SHE

He's actually lost a lot of weight.

A pause.

HE

You saw him?

SHE

No. I weighed him. Yes, I saw him.

HE

What did you say?

SHE

I didn't say anything. I just saw him. He was walking in the street, and I was walking on the other side and I saw him.

HE

And he saw you.

SHE

If he did, he didn't say anything.

HE

And you noticed how svelte he was. How now, in this slimmed state, he could squeeze round any table he liked.

SHE

At the time, I had no idea how little space I would have in the future.

HE

And is this the future?
(*beat*)
I don't want to put that table in this room.

A pause.

I want a new table.

SHE

But what about the old one?

HE

We'll sell it.

SHE

To whom?

HE

I don't know. Someone who needs a table.

SHE

We need a table.

HE

We don't need this table.

SHE

We don't need this room.

HE

There's nothing wrong with the room.

SHE

What is it for?

A beat.

HE

It's a dining room.

SHE

A dining room needs a table.

HE

Not that one.

A pause.

It's me or the table.

SHE

The table or you.

HE

That's right.

SHE

And where am I?

HE

What's this?

SHE

Where am I?

Freeze.

Tableau.

Lights fade.

They fade back up.

The room now contains an extremely large table.

Crouching under the table is a man with his back to us. This is SEBASTIAN.

He produces a violin and begins to play Handel's Partita in C minor.

He and She stare out at us.

We cut to black.

ROAST

Introduction
by Lady Virginia Lovilocke

Harauld's wonderful *Roast* will always have a place in my heart. It was the first play of his that I saw live (the famous 1974 revival), and though we were not then married, I knew that we were destined to play a profound part in one another's lives. Harauld said that he saw me appear like a shining angel in the audience, and the light from my spirit had pierced his heart, which was sweet of him to mention. He later wrote me a poem:

> 'Light'
>
> The light
> From your
> Angel eyes
> Has pierced
> My sides.

When I asked him why he changed 'heart' to 'sides', his entire face darkened and his voice lowered to the most profound bass. 'Do you like the poem or not?' he said. I told him I liked it very much, but it was a little short. He left the room in search of a pen. When he returned, he thrust another stanza into my hand:

> Behind my
> Curtained place
> I watched you
> Beam and I
> Dove in
> And drowned.

I said, 'Harauld, where were you? It's been two days. The police are here.'

'Do you like it or not?' he asked. I cried, and he held me and told the investigating officers to go because he had to make love to me immediately.

Of course, *Roast* is not just about a roast lunch, though Harauld did love roasts, and I made him one every Sunday, no matter where in the world we were. He once told me, his mouth glazed with lamb, that if there weren't roasts like mine in heaven, he didn't want to go. I said, 'Don't worry, Harauld, there's no way you're going to heaven.'

And he liked that very much.

Roast premiered at the Royal Court in 1962 and ran for a year before anyone could catch it. The original cast was as follows:

PETE	Mick Barrett
MICK	Crispin Kelp
CHARLIE	Tony Dunlop

The cast for the version filmed for *The Harauld Hughes Half-Hour Play* was as follows:

PETE	Crispin Kelp
MICK	Arden Hall
CHARLIE	'Kippy' Mank
HARAULD HUGHES	Himself
ACTRESS/PRINCESS	Inger Marie
ACTOR	Edmund Butterby

INT. STAGE

A bare stage.

HARAULD HUGHES is dressed in black.

He finds the light.

He addresses us.

> HARAULD
>
> My name is Harauld Hughes. I'm a playwright. It's a curse I have to live with. People ask me to explain my plays. I tell them that everything they need to know about the play is already in the play. And then they ask, 'Is that why it's so hard to find out information about when your plays are on?' And I say, 'Maybe. I don't know. What are words?'

Enter an ACTRESS.

> ACTRESS
>
> A word is a bullet. It can pierce your heart.

Enter an ACTOR.

> ACTOR
>
> But is a bullet a word?

Harauld turns quickly.

> HARAULD
>
> Bang!

The Actor looks down at his chest, then looks up. His eyes go wide. He falls to his knees. He falls back.

CUT TO:

EXT. DREAM SPACE

Harauld is there to catch him.

Harauld holds the Actor in his arms.

They are now in a strange, black field.

HARAULD

Shh! Shh! It won't be long now. The word went clean through your heart.

The wind starts up.

ACTOR

Cold, so cold.

HARAULD

You should've worn a jacket.

ACTOR

Can I have yours?

HARAULD

But then *I'll* be cold.

ACTOR

But I'm dying.

HARAULD

Exactly. How can a jacket save you?

ACTOR

Don't you want to make me comfortable before I die?

HARAULD

I'm the one who needs to be comfortable, I've got to go on living.

A Pre-Raphaelite PRINCESS appears, on a horse.

PRINCESS

You must let Harauld be comfortable.

HARAULD
(*shouting, to the Actress*)
I've done all I can!

PRINCESS
No one could do more. You must be drained!

HARAULD
My characters demand so much of me.

PRINCESS
You must preserve your strength for your writing.

ACTOR
I'm sorry for asking so much of you, Harauld. It wasn't fair.

HARAULD
Do you see now? Do you see how dangerous words can be?

The Actor dies in his arms.

PRINCESS
Without you, he has nothing to say.

HARAULD
I couldn't give him my jacket.

PRINCESS
You gave him life; you've every right to keep your jacket.

HARAULD
It *is* my jacket.

PRINCESS
Do not reproach yourself. There are too many actors.

HARAULD
Why are there so many of them?

PRINCESS
Come. Let me return you to the well.

HARAULD

My creative well.

The Princess laughs.

PRINCESS

From what other well wouldst thou drink?!

She laughs again.

CUT TO:

EXT. GLADE

A well at its centre.

In the field, many actors/actresses running around. Each one says one word again and again.

HARAULD

I have been away from the well for so long. I barely recognise it.

PRINCESS

Words have got in the way.

HARAULD

They always do.

PRINCESS

Your well is pure and deeper than language.

HARAULD

Thank you.

He nods in acknowledgement of the depth of his well.

PRINCESS

Go to it. Drink, slake your tongue and replenish your spirit.

HARAULD

Will you kiss me before I go?

PRINCESS

I don't think that would be appropriate. For I am you. And
you cannot kiss yourself.

HARAULD

Can we at least try?

The Princess rides off.

*Harauld walks determinedly through the fields of buzzing
words, until he reaches the well.*

He looks down into the well.

He lets down the bucket and then pulls it up.

*Just as he's about to drink, a hand comes out and grabs him by
the throat.*

He manages to free himself, falling to his knees.

He falls back out of frame . . .

CUT TO:

INT. THEATRE

. . . and into the arms of the Princess, now dressed as an Actress.

HARAULD

Where am I?

ACTRESS

A theatre. Your theatre.

HARAULD

Who is at the table?

We see a table, against black.

Three actors look round. They are holding scripts.

ACTRESS

Actors.

HARAULD

And they have . . . the words.

ACTRESS

Yes. They have your words.

HARAULD

Then I am . . . where I should be.

ACTRESS

Yes. You are . . .

HARAULD

Home.

(*beat*)

Will you kiss me now?

ACTRESS

Yes.

We cut to black.

Caption: 'ROAST'.

CUT TO:

INT. STAGE

A room, sparsely furnished. A kitchen is offstage right. There's a door at the back of the room.

PETE (30s) and CHARLIE (30s) sit in a room. A few chairs. A bed in one corner. Pete is reading the paper. Charlie stares into the middle distance.

A long pause.

PETE

It's disgusting. What's going on.

CHARLIE

How do you know what's going on?

PETE

Says here, doesn't it?

CHARLIE

What does it say?

PETE

It says it all.

CHARLIE

All?

PETE

It's all laid out.

CHARLIE

You don't have a clue.

PETE

How would you know?

CHARLIE

How would I know what?

PETE

What a clue was.

CHARLIE

You wouldn't know where to start.

PETE

I've got more clues than I know what to do with. I'm up to my neck in them.

CHARLIE

And whence do these clues emanate?

PETE

Whence? What's whence?

CHARLIE

Whence. 'From where'.

PETE

Then why don't you say 'from where'?

CHARLIE

Because 'whence' is shorter. 'Whence' is the contraction.

PETE

Well, it's not contracted this exchange, has it, mate? It's made it longer. It's dragged the arse out of it.

CHARLIE

All right. Then allow me to rephrase. From where do these clues emanate?

PETE

What's 'emanate'?

CHARLIE

You don't have the vocabulary for this dialogue, do you? You lack the basic syntactic competence to converse. You don't have a proper grounding. That's your problem, mate. You're afloat. You've got no anchor. You're without bearings. You have no idea where you are. You're irredeemably adrift. You're lost, mate.

PETE

You talk too much.

CHARLIE

I've got to make sense for the both of us. That's why.

PETE

I know where I am. Don't you worry about it. I know exactly where I'm at.

CHARLIE

And where's that?

PETE

Right here.

CHARLIE

Right here?

PETE

Right here, mate!

CHARLIE

Where's here?

PETE

I don't need to say. It's clear as day.

CHARLIE

You don't have a clue.

PETE

I'm going to sleep.

CHARLIE

How will I tell?

Pete walks over to the bed and lies down.

Charlie picks up the paper and leafs through it.

Disgusting.

Enter MICK, a man in his 50s/60s.

MICK

Well?

CHARLIE

Well what?

MICK

Is that all I get?

CHARLIE

Were you expecting more?

MICK

I should know better by now.

CHARLIE

What should you know?

MICK

Better. I should know better. What's wrong with you?

CHARLIE

How can you know something better? You either know it
or you don't.

MICK

You're binary. That's your downfall. It's got to be either
this or that.

CHARLIE

Well, what else can it be?

MICK

Neither this *nor* that.

CHARLIE

If it's not *this* and it's not *that*, what is it?

Pete rises from his bed.

PETE

The other. It's the other.

CHARLIE

Who asked you, Pete?

They stare at one another.

MICK

How many fathers you got?

CHARLIE

Not this.

MICK

Go on.

CHARLIE

How many fathers does anyone have?

PETE

Depends on the person.

CHARLIE

He's not talking to you, is he?

94

PETE

I'm awake now.

CHARLIE

He didn't ask you. He asked me.

PETE

So why don't you answer?

CHARLIE

I've given my answer. Obliquely.

MICK

Don't be oblique to your father.

PETE

What's 'oblique'?

CHARLIE

Read a book, Pete.

PETE

I read. I read all about it.

CHARLIE

I'll be as oblique as I like.

MICK

If you want to be oblique, if you want to be opaque, get your own place. But this is my house, and in this house we're explicitly transparent. And don't you two turds forget it.

CHARLIE

Mum left this house to me. I'm the eldest.

MICK

How could Mum leave this house to you? She's not dead. Plus, it's not hers! She's not on the deeds. She's got no legal hold over the premises.

CHARLIE

If Mum's not dead, where is she?

PETE

Leave it, Charlie.

CHARLIE

No, you leave it, Petey.

MICK

She's popped out.

CHARLIE

Oh. Popped out, has she?

MICK

Yes. She's got the right, hasn't she? She's got the right to pop out.

CHARLIE

Longest pop-out I've ever heard of.

PETE

Charlie . . .

CHARLIE

I'm warning you, I'll bury you. I'll cover you in soil. Where's she popped out to then?

MICK

She's popped out for some bits and bobs.

CHARLIE

For some bits?

PETE

And bobs, Charlie.

MICK

For the roast.

PETE

Mum does a lovely roast.

MICK

Every Sunday. She knows her boys. She knows what they need.

PETE

We get hungry, don't we, Dad?

MICK

Who knows that more than Mum? She knows just how
hungry we can get.

PETE

I get so hungry, Dad.

MICK

I know you do, Petey. That's why Mum's put the oven on.
So the meat can crisp.

CHARLIE

I suppose there'll be gravy too?

MICK

Course there'll be gravy. What do you take your mum for?
A slut?

PETE

Mum always does gravy. She knows how we like it. Right
up to the brim of the boat.

MICK

Why wouldn't there be gravy, Charlie? Answer me that.
You think your mother's a whore? You think she's too
busy selling her body to make a hot sauce for her boys?
You think she'd serve up a dry slab and expect us to
swallow it?

PETE

Won't there be gravy, Dad? I can't have it without gravy.

MICK

Mum wouldn't even plate up unless the gravy boat was
steaming. That must be why she popped out. She probably
needs something for the gravy.

CHARLIE

Really? Bits for the gravy?

PETE

It's not just bits, Charlie, it's also bobs. Tell him, Dad.

CHARLIE

Sod your bobs, Petey. Stick your bobs right up your arsehole. She don't need anything for the gravy. The roast itself provides the gravy. It's all there from the juices. That's the gravy. You don't need any bits. You just need to drain off the juice.

MICK

There's more to it than that.

CHARLIE

You ever made a gravy?

MICK

Course I haven't. That's Mum's domain. She'd kill me.

CHARLIE

Then shut up about it.

PETE

Don't you tell Dad to shut up.

CHARLIE

Then tell him to stop talking so much shit about the gravy.

Pause. A stand-off.

MICK

There's all sorts in that gravy. Stuff you wouldn't believe.

PETE

Don't you ever tell this beautiful man to shut up. No one's eaten more roasts than him. He's had one every Sunday of his life.

MICK

It sets me up for the week.

PETE

You want to learn some appreciation. A sense of where you come from. A sense of obligation.

CHARLIE

You don't know what obligation is.

PETE

I know what I owe.

CHARLIE

So do I. I clear my plate.

PETE

Do you?

CHARLIE

My slate is clean.

PETE

When you wanted to retrain as an accountant, who did you go to? After you spaffed it all trying to be a skydiver. We told you there was no money in it.

MICK

There's no money in it, Charlie.

PETE

You said, 'Let me find out.' You jacked it all in. To become a skydiver. Only it's not a job. It's not an actual job, is it?

CHARLIE

It's not a job *yet*.

PETE

It'll never be a job. There's no need. There's no one needs a skydiver on a regular basis.

CHARLIE

It's still early days.

PETE

In fact, it's the other way round. You've got to pay to skydive. You're losing money. All the time. Hand over fist. You may as well chuck the money out the plane.

CHARLIE

But that's the thing, Petey. To whom am I losing money?

PETE

You're dumping it out the cargo doors, mate.

CHARLIE

But who's getting the money?

PETE

It's not you, that's for sure. It's not you, is it, Charlie boy?

MICK

Go easy, son, he's fragile.

CHARLIE

It's not just the pilot up there, you know . . .

PETE

Co-pilot, is there?

CHARLIE

There's no co-pilot to speak of. It's not that scale of plane.

PETE

How would I know the scale? What would I know about that?

CHARLIE

Put your mind to it.

PETE

It's not my area.

MICK

He has other interests, Charlie.

CHARLIE

So, who else is there? Who else is up there?

A pause.

You can do it, Pete. It's within your purview.

MICK

He hasn't dwelt on the matter, Charlie.

CHARLIE

Keep the rope taut.

MICK

He needs more time. You can't artificially accelerate the processes of cognition.

PETE

An instructor.

CHARLIE

There he is.

PETE

You've got an instructor with you.

MICK

You just needed time, didn't you, Petey?

PETE

I can't think right away. I never could.

CHARLIE

An instructor. Do you see now? Do you see where I'm coming from? I could be an instructor. I could introduce skydiving to the next generation. I could be part of a rich pedagogical lineage.

A pause.

MICK

You call that a job? Instructing?

CHARLIE

What else do you call it?

MICK

I call it a shame. A man, strapped to another man.

CHARLIE

You're never strapped. You're in a hold.

MICK

A man, on top of another man. Falling. That's not a job. That's a predicament.

CHARLIE

There's going to be money in it. Just you wait. Good money.

MICK

What comes of it? A job's got to be necessary or it's not a job. Clean out the oven. That's a job. Drop a case up the Elephant. That's a job.

PETE

Responsibly filing your tax returns. That's a job.

CHARLIE

I don't want to be an accountant. I want to skydive.

MICK

Someone with your mind shouldn't be rapidly descending through the firmament like some kind of ejected Icarus. You should be employing your faculties in the financial sector.

CHARLIE

I feel free in the sky.

MICK

We're not made for the sky. It's a waste of life.

CHARLIE

So's accountancy.

MICK

Thank fuck Mum's not hearing this. You call reducing people's overall tax burdens a waste? How else are companies meant to keep accurate records of their dealings? How are stakeholders, investors, regulators and managers meant to know what in fuck* is going on without accurate accounting?

PETE

It's the language of business, Charlie.

---

* A note on the language: in the original, the word 'fuck' was replaced by 'heck' or similar.

CHARLIE

What would you know about the language of business?
You're a florist.

PETE

We've got a till.

CHARLIE

A bucket is not a till.

PETE

A till is anywhere you put the money.

CHARLIE

A till's got a little drawer that pops out and goes ping.

PETE

The only thing that's popped out round here is Mum.

CHARLIE

Mum's not popped out. She's gone. She popped out five
years ago. That's when I started skydiving. Only it wasn't
skydiving. I wanted to die. I was going to do myself in,
wasn't I? I was going to end it. I wasn't going to open the
parachute. But then I saw Mum. She was in the sky. She
was in the air beneath me. She was all around me. She
told me to live. There were tears in my eyes. 'I can't go on
without you,' I told her. 'We've lost our rock.' She said she
had to go, she couldn't stay by that stove for the rest of her
life. She had to go. She was happy now. She could breathe.
There was more to life than putting the roast on. There *are*
other things to eat. It doesn't always have to be a roast.
'Don't be like me,' she said. 'Don't serve up something if
you haven't got the stomach for it.' And that's when I saw
it. I knew. I was flying. I was me.

MICK

You're off your nut. You're not well.

PETE

You need to eat.

MICK

He gets like this when he's hungry. He needs feeding up.

PETE

He needs a roast.

MICK

Mum'll see to that. She'll watch him clear his plate.

PETE

When will she be back?

MICK

Soon, Petey. Soon.

Pete goes back to his paper.

Mick exits back into the kitchen.

Charlie sits back down.

Slow fade.

ROOST

Introduction
by Augustus Pink

'After an all-male *Roast*, in which the absent voices of women form a ghostly counterpoint to the pronounced and apoplectic braggadocio, *Roost* foregrounds the feminine.' So ran the opening line of my review, written but an hour after the rapturous applause that marked the final tableau of the latest Hughes production. An hour after publication, I received a telegram: 'The feminine does not reside on an axis. Yours, Harauld.'

I was well rebuked. Though indisputably a feminist, despite what women seem to say, Hughes refused to emphasise any one aspect of his work over another, let alone give it a gendered tilt. It is the perfect balance of elements – from the compression of the badinage to the diffusion of the lighting, from the heft of a jacket to the lightness of the interval refreshments (chosen by Hughes to complement the drama) – that is the Hughesian hallmark. Everything is in the service of Truth, even, and perhaps especially, untruth.

The deliberately similar titles of the two plays, *Roast* and *Roost*, with only a varying diphthong to differentiate them, bind them together like twins. As Hughes remarked, 'Before a roast, something's got to roost.' In *Roost*, the repast of choice is stew, but a stew of memory, an Edenic concoction made by another absent mother. Perhaps 'stew of memory' is as good a way of describing Hughes's work as any other. Of his own mother, Hughes said, 'I never met her, but they say she could burn water.' So was this idealised offstage caregiver a wish fulfilment? Some say she was a projection, given final flesh in the figure of Lady Virginia Lovilocke, the celebrated theologian and chef, who would become Hughes's final wife. As Hughes remarked, 'I don't think I'd ever eaten till I'd been fed by her.'

It is an irony, then, that in *Roost* the part of 'Vivian', who claims to 'cook all the time', was originated by Harauld's first wife, Felicity Stoat, a woman whose only chance of making a meal of something was to be given the closing speech before the Act Two curtain. A capable performer, nothing suited her better than the role of the Hughesian woman. Regrettably, she started to feel that she was being mined, used for material, in a complete misunderstanding of how art transforms and ultimately supersedes life. Her continual carping could have been a source of conflict, had Hughes not been distracted by his numerous affairs. Stoat's ingratitude must have taken a toll on him, but, nevertheless, she is an inescapable part of the Hughes canon. All the major female roles in these theatre works were originated by her (though the more comely Inger Marie tended to take her parts on screen), and she remained relatively sexy well into her mid-thirties, a true achievement for a heavy smoker.

I did have the misfortune to eat at her table, but mercifully only once. She did, indeed, manage to burn the water.

Roost was first performed at the Royal Court in 1962. The original cast was as follows:

TERRY	Mick Barrett
MICK	Arden Hall
VIVIAN	Felicity Stoat
MILKMAN/GORDON	Edmund Butterby

The cast for the version filmed for *The Harauld Hughes Half-Hour Play* was as follows:

HARAULD HUGHES	Himself
TERRY	Patrick Rusk
MICK/PRIEST	Arden Hall
VIVIAN/WOMAN 1	Inger Marie
MILKMAN/GORDON/ACTOR	Edmund Butterby
ACTRESS/MOTHER/WOMAN 8	Felicity Stoat
WOMAN 2	Dinki Gustavsson
WOMAN 3	Babs Plank
WOMAN 4	Honey Graves
WOMAN 5	Binty Frisk
WOMAN 6	Jackie Jarvis
WOMAN 7	Ivory Steele

INT. STAGE

A bare stage.

HARAULD HUGHES is dressed in black.

He finds the light.

He addresses us.

>   HARAULD
> My name is Harauld Hughes. I write plays. I don't analyse
> them. I despise the word 'analyse'. I refuse all categories.
> There is no right nor wrong; only what is. Which is both.

Enter an ACTOR from the wings.

>   ACTOR
> And neither.

>   HARAULD
> Well said, old friend.

>   ACTOR
> Is not 'friend' just another category?

>   HARAULD
> No. It is a promise. A promise to fail.

Enter an ACTRESS.

>   ACTRESS
> Is that why you failed me?

>   HARAULD
> Yes. Because I am your friend.

>   ACTRESS
> Can a man be a friend?

HARAULD

In my plays, there is no such thing as A Man. There is
no such thing as A Woman. There are only Actors. And,
occasionally, Actresses.

*The Actress enters Harauld's frame. There is a stab of frightening
music.*

ACTRESS

Do women scare you, Harauld?

HARAULD

I love women.

CUT TO:

INT. PHOTOGRAPHER'S STUDIO

*Eight WOMEN, against a mottled backdrop, a little like a
school photo.*

Harauld, in front, sitting in a director's chair.

WOMAN 1

Do you love me, Harauld?

A spotlight switches on and focuses on Harauld.

*As the following exchanges progress, the light on Harauld gets
brighter and brighter.*

HARAULD

Yes.

WOMAN 2

Do you love me, Harauld?

HARAULD

Yes.

WOMAN 3

Do you love me, Harauld?

HARAULD

Yes.

WOMAN 4

Do you love me, Harauld?

HARAULD

Yes.

WOMAN 5

Do you love me, Harauld?

HARAULD

Yes.

WOMAN 6

Do you love me, Harauld?

HARAULD

Yes.

WOMAN 7

Do you love me, Harauld?

HARAULD

Yes.

WOMAN 8

Do you love me, Harauld?

HARAULD

Yes.

CUT TO:

EXT. LAKE − DUSK

The eight women stand on the shore.

HARAULD

Do you, in turn, love me?

*He is in a boat, drifting away. He looks behind him. His
MOTHER (an unloving nun) is rowing the boat.*

He sees the women recede.

HARAULD

Do you, in turn, love me?!

WOMEN

No, Harauld.

HARAULD

Did any one of you ever love me?

They recede further.

Harauld turns to his Mother; though a nun and a mother, she is very attractive.

MOTHER

There's no one on God's earth who can replace your mother, Harauld.

HARAULD

Mother, did you ever love me?

But she is gone.

Harauld is alone, drifting in the boat on the lake.

Smoke starts to drift through the frame.

We cut to a young Harauld on a bicycle (played by the adult Harauld – perhaps in shorts?), cycling as fast as he can across a kind of scrubland.

He gets to a clearing, where a fire rages ahead.

In front is a barricade, hastily assembled and manned by some soldiers.

Young Harauld screeches to a halt and leaves his bicycle to fall.

He runs towards the fire but is intercepted by a soldier, who hoists him into the air.

At the base of the fire, his Mother. She turns round and stares at him.

On her other side, a PRIEST. He is holding the Mother in a way that does not seem appropriate.

Young Harauld looks up, and on top of the pyre, strapped to a stake, is Adult Harauld, sweat dripping from his forehead.

Young Harauld screams.

We cut close to Adult Harauld, on top of the pyre.

CUT TO:

INT. STAGE

Adult Harauld, in close-up. Sweat on his brow, eyes closed.

The frame brightens and becomes white.

CUT TO:

Play title: 'ROOST'.

CUT TO:

INT. A ROOM – EARLY MORNING

A man, TERRY (40s), enters a room. He holds the door open for a woman, VIVIAN (30s/40s), his wife.

Terry switches on a light. The room is sparsely furnished: two armchairs, a low table, a standard lamp towards the back. It's a basement room, with the light coming from the rear through metal security bars. To the right, the entrance to a kitchen.

> TERRY
>
> So, what do you think?

> VIVIAN
>
> Not much.

TERRY

I meant about the room.

VIVIAN

I'm getting my bearings.

TERRY

You're orientating yourself.

VIVIAN

I said what I'm doing. I'm getting my bearings.

TERRY

It's the same thing.

VIVIAN

Then why do you ask?

From the kitchen to the side, a noise.

Enter a muscular man, MICK (50s). He is not wearing a shirt, only a vest.

MICK

She's not Mum, is she?

TERRY

No.

A pause.

I realised that almost immediately.

MICK

This one is completely different. She's a different prospect altogether. Does she cook?

VIVIAN

Yes, quite well. To a high standard, actually.

TERRY

I don't know. I've never asked her.

VIVIAN

I cook all the time. I never stop. Sometimes I wish I could stop. But I don't.

MICK

Christ, Mum could cook. If she did you a stew, you knew about it.

TERRY

Melted in the mouth.

MICK

You barely had to chew.

TERRY

It wasn't mush, though.

MICK

Was it fuck.* You've got the wrong idea if you think Mum's stews went to mush. If you think they were like soup, you're cracked. Each chunk of meat was firm on the fork. It had a texture. It told a story.

A pause.

Take her coat off. Let's see what we're dealing with.

Terry takes off Vivian's coat.

She's not like Mum.

TERRY

I know.

MICK

Doesn't say much, does she?

VIVIAN

To speak to people, to see through their eyes, to hold between us the invisible thread of language, a connection perhaps more precious for being so fine, is one of life's greatest joys.

MICK

I don't mind them vacant. Saves me the earache.

---

* A note on the language: in the original, the word 'fuck' was replaced by the sound of a car's engine.

117

TERRY

She's enigmatic. Like Mum was.

MICK

She's fuck all like Mum.

TERRY

I know. I know that now.

MICK

There's nothing to her. She's like a mist.

TERRY

I meant that they're similar in their unknowability.

MICK

That's not a similarity. Unknowability is not a quality.
It's an absence. It's like saying two dead people share the
property of non-being. It's not enough to go on.

VIVIAN

Terry rather tends to transpose his own cognitive
incapacities into a purported characteristic of the person
he's talking to. It's one of the reasons I've never had a
climax with him.

Mick continues, as if he hasn't heard Vivian.

MICK

I suggest you refrain from transposing your own cognitive
incapacities into a purported characteristic of the person
you're talking to. Little tip for you.

TERRY

Sorry.

MICK

Don't apologise. Take a moment to reckon with yourself.

TERRY

The apology is my attempt to reckon with myself.

MICK

It's boring. It's bogus. It's pat.

A pause.

TERRY

Couldn't you think of another adjective that begins with 'b'?

MICK

I know plenty of adjectives that begin with 'b'.

TERRY

Name one.

MICK

'Bright'. But it didn't apply.

A pause.

You don't know how to get people to open up, do you? You never could. Not that I've seen. You've got no friends. I can't think of a single person who regards you with fondness.

TERRY

I have friends.

MICK

Name one.

TERRY

Gordon.

MICK

Gordon hates you. He absolutely hates you.

TERRY

Gordon's a prick.

MICK

I thought he was your mate.

TERRY

We fell out.

Mick indicates Vivian.

MICK

Does she always look this tired? She needs a cup of tea. To revive her. Terry, make her a cup of tea.

TERRY

You know where the kitchen is.

MICK

What's that got to do with it?

TERRY

Why don't you make her a cup of tea?

MICK

Because I'm busy. Or are you too thick to see how busy I am?

He stares at Terry.

VIVIAN

Tea makes me sick. Something to do with the way the caffeine is absorbed into the blood. I can have coffee, but never tea.

MICK

Make it nice and milky. With sugar.

Terry leaves. Mick looks at Vivian.

You think you're better than me. Is that it? I'm lucky just to look at you, is that it?

VIVIAN

We've been touring Europe for the last few months. Like Montaigne, we left our walled enclosure and sought to encounter the world and its riches. I thought our journey might stimulate some discussion – a rebirth – between my husband and I. A deeper . . . understanding. I can only give myself to a man if the man first gives himself to me. Unconditionally, without reservation. But Terry, I've discovered, is an empty shell, signifying nothing, rarely emitting a sound, let alone fury. He has nothing left. He has poured his meagre essence into his work. I cannot respect any man who works. Work repels me – its incessant need for timetabling, its triviality, its counterfeit promise of redemption. And the funny thing is, he thinks his work is important. 'Vivian.' My name is Vivian. 'Vivian,' he says, 'I'm a paediatric surgeon.' 'Terrence,' I say – I like to make his name longer, 'Terry' sounds like a mouse – 'Terrence,' I say, 'if saving children's lives is so important to you, why have a wife?' Terrence counters, without reflection, 'But we can have children of our own.' I reply, 'I'd rather die than have your filth inside me. If we ever had a child, I would eat it whole.'

Mick turns and shouts off.

MICK

Why won't she talk?

Terry calls from off.

TERRY

I can't hear you. The kettle's steaming. It's Mum's favourite kettle. Remember? The grey one. The loud greeny-grey one. With the extra-wide nozzle. Mum loved that extra-wide nozzle. Amount of tea she made, she needed it.

Vivian looks out, addressing no one in particular in a calm, narration-style voice.

At the same time, we hear the increasingly high-pitched sound of the kettle.

VIVIAN

I was calm as a child. It was only later that I realised I was anxious. Or perhaps it was the other way round. And I find myself having the kind of encounters now that I should have had in adolescence. I find myself in the grip of romantic obsessions – crushes – a desire – for there is no other word, not even 'lust' with its monosyllabically assonant thrust – a desire for the purely masculine. Its brutality. Its narrowness. Its urgency. A compulsion to satisfy has become my only satisfaction. An engulfing fire. I burn with a heat that can only dim in the daze that follows the brazen animalistic rut of conjoining.

She turns and addresses Mick directly, looking right at him.

VIVIAN

But only with the right man. I can only give myself to a man who knows himself. Who knows his power. His force. Such a man need only ask. Mick – I'll call you Michael, it's longer – do you know of such a man?

MICK

She's just standing here. Schtum. Inviolable. Like a totem. Like an edifice. It's agitating me. I can feel a sense of rising agitation.

Vivian slowly turns back to face the audience.

Terry comes in with the tea.

Is this what she's like? Is this what we're contending with? A brick wall?

He takes the tea.

TERRY

I don't know. We've only been married three years.

MICK

I like a bit of conversation. It passes the time.

He drinks the tea in one gulp, like it's a pint.

He grimaces.

TERRY

What the hell do you call that?

MICK

Cup of tea.

TERRY

It's black as night. It's like brine. It's practically Baltic.

MICK

You're out of milk.

TERRY

There's milk on the side.

MICK

That milk's solid. It's impermeable. It's like a new microclimate. It's biodiverse.

TERRY

Well, pop to the shop.

MICK

You pop to the shop.

A pause.

I need a tea, Tel. I'm parched.

TERRY

That was the last of it.

MICK

I'm gasping, Tel. My tongue's like the Mojave.

TERRY

Have a glass of water.

MICK

We're on the verge of an altercation, Tel. We're perilously close to a bust-up.

TERRY

Have a glass of water.

MICK

I won't. You can't make me. I haven't drunk water since I was a boy.

TERRY

That's your lookout. I'm here now. I've just arrived. I'm here with my new wife.

MICK

I thought you'd been married three years.

TERRY

She's new to you, though.

MICK

You don't know what's new to me.

TERRY

You're new to her.

MICK

Pop. To. The. Shop.

TERRY

Why do you need so much milk, Mick?

MICK

I need so much milk, Tel, because I'm such a big boy. Now run out and fetch it.

Silence.

There's a knock at the door.

After a stand-off, Terry leaves the room and walks to the front door.

He opens the door.

There, with a bottle of milk in his hand, is the MILKMAN.

MILKMAN

Your milk, sir. You want to take it in sharpish. There's a lot of sticky fingers round here.

TERRY

I happen to like the area. It's up-and-coming.

MILKMAN

There are some places, and this is one of them, that have always been, and will always be, a shithole.

The Milkman keeps looking at Terry. Vivian walks out with him.

She turns and looks at Terry.

Vivian and the Milkman leave together.

Terry comes back in with the milk.

> MICK

Who was that?

> TERRY

Gordon.

> MICK

Gordon? I thought you fell out.

> TERRY

We did.

> MICK

Did he mention anything?

> TERRY

No. He was just there. With the milk.

> MICK

Where's your wife?

> TERRY

She went with Gordon.

> MICK

She never had her tea.

> TERRY

No. She never did.

> MICK

There was something about her that was unresolved.

> TERRY

Did you detect a wound?

> MICK

I did. I detected a hurt.

TERRY

A defensiveness?

MICK

If you like.

TERRY

Her family came from money. But they lost it all.

MICK

Business people, were they?

TERRY

Packaging. They were packing magnates. Then they packed it in.

MICK

Cartons and so forth.

TERRY

Long life.

MICK

I thought her dad hanged himself.

TERRY

No. The packaging's long-life. Milk. UHT, they call it.

MICK

UHT?

TERRY

It's an acronym.

MICK

No, it's not.

TERRY

Yes, it is. UHT stands for something.

MICK

If UHT were an acronym, it'd be pronounced 'uht'. Scuba is an acronym. An acronym is when the first letters of a series of words spell out a new one. Self-contained underwater breathing apparatus. Scuba. I know an acronym when I see one. UHT is an initialism. Three ugly letters, made uglier by the stinking honk of your unrefined voice.

TERRY

Ultra-Heat-Treated. Kills everything.

MICK

It's not for me. I need a breeze. I've got to have the window open or I can't breathe.

TERRY

Maybe you should wear a scuba suit.

MICK

In the house?

A pause.

Your wife's a whore.

TERRY

She's a leading professor of linguistics at one of the most prestigious universities in America.

MICK

Still ran off with the milkman, though.

TERRY

She'll be back.

MICK

Back where, Tel? You don't live here, so you won't be here, will you?

TERRY

You kicking me out?

MICK

You already left, mate. Left me and Mum on our own. I never had a brother, growing up.

TERRY

I left three years ago.

MICK

You left us. Left us to fend for ourselves.

TERRY

You're in your fifties, Mick. Your late fifties.

MICK

It still hurts, though.

TERRY

You're much older than me.

MICK

You left us, Terry. And now Mum's dead.

TERRY

She died before I left.

MICK

That doesn't bring her back, though, does it?

Silence.

TERRY

What would?

MICK

And you certainly can't replace Mum with a whore. I don't care how big her tits are. Because once a woman's got a house by the scruff of its neck, that's *finito*. Take it from me. Take that up the Aldwych.

A pause.

I think you should fuck off now.

TERRY

Unless I were to stay?

MICK

Here?

TERRY

Where else?

MICK

In this room?

TERRY

I'd pay my way.

MICK

You'd have to. The area's up-and-coming.

TERRY

Is that what they're saying?

MICK

Just you and me?

TERRY

Who else?

MICK

We used to share this room, didn't we, Tel?

TERRY

When we were boys.

MICK

Back from the game.

TERRY

Full of drink.

MICK

Wet from the shower.

TERRY

Mum's got the tea on.

MICK

She's on the warpath.

TERRY

We'll soften her up.

MICK

We'll smooth her brow.

TERRY

We'll tickle her feet.

MICK

We'll kiss her cheek.

TERRY

And what'll she say?

MICK

The usual.

TERRY

What she always says?

MICK

What else?

TERRY

Will you say it, Mick? Say it like she would.

MICK

'My boys are back. They've come home. They've come home to roost.'

Mick takes the milk. He takes the cap off the bottle.

He begins to drink.

We hear a knocking from the front door.

The knocking becomes increasingly insistent.

We snap to black.

PROMPT

Introduction
by Leslie Francis

It is perhaps fitting that I should introduce Harauld's teleplay of *Prompt*. After all, I appear in it. Or, rather, a version of what claims to be me appears in it. And, further, we might divide this version or claim into three parts: Harauld's claim as the writer of *Prompt* about the character Leslie Francis (the director) in *Prompt*; my claim as Leslie Francis (the director of *Prompt*) about the text of *Prompt* as written by Harauld; and my claim as Leslie Francis (the actor in *Prompt*) playing the director Leslie Francis. The interplay between these different truth claims is one of the things that gives the work such vitality.

It was as a director that I had hitherto worked with Harauld. I had directed his first play, *Platform*, for the stage and found an immediate ally in terms of sensibility, if not temperament. Harauld was from the lower classes, and like many autodidacts, his education hardly lacked for lacunae. But he had an actor's ear for dialogue and a ragamuffin's sense of the street.

And it was this 'street sense' that seemed to govern his conduct: an uneasy mix of (in my view) tokenistic loyalty mixed with arbitrary brutality. It was terribly attractive, especially for someone (like me) who had boarded from a young age. His masculine qualities were transfixing; he loved sports and would thrash me at badminton with a relish that always bucked the spirit. He showered openly and with no self-consciousness, finishing each douche in a great cloud of aggressively applied talc. It was without the slightest trace of solicitousness that he would ask me to towel the small of his back. It was simply what friends did to avoid getting a rash. I wonder if he knew the agonies of my soul?

Our rehearsals for *The Harauld Hughes Half-Hour Play* were short and often pressured, as we could work only at night, when the studios were free. I sometimes wonder whether what came to be known as the 'Hughesian Howl' was simply our attempt to compete with the noise of industrial cleaning equipment. I invited Harauld to attend the rehearsals (a courtesy I extend to all my writers), and Harauld, who liked to drink, would swing by after one of his debauches and start to inveigh.

Like St John before him, Harauld believed in the supremacy of The Word; but unlike St John, Harauld seemed to think that *he* was The Way, The Truth and The Light. The text was sacred and not to be questioned. Each comma was a hill on which he was willing to die, even if it originated as a typo. I've never met a man who trusted himself so utterly. His plays, he would say, were not written, they were channelled, and he had no more business questioning them than the weather.

Harauld was, at heart, a surrealist. His plays erupted out of his subconscious; that is the privilege of the writer. I am not a writer. I am a director. And if I have a heart, it is that of a symbolist. I believe that a director must use comprehensible signs as a way of transmitting his intention to an audience, and for that he must use his conscious faculties, or else he's sunk. Harauld couldn't explain himself, but I had to explain Harauld to the crew. This could lead to some fearsome rows:

Harauld: That's not what I meant!
Me: Then what do you mean?
Harauld: That's none of your business!
Me: What you mean is the basis of my business.
Harauld: I'm ambivalent about business.
Me: I can't film ambivalence. I need certainty.
Harauld: Certainty is not the antonym of ambivalence.
Me: It literally is.
Harauld: That's not what I meant!
Me: You mean so very little.

And so on . . .

It hurt me a pinch more than I cared to admit that Harauld stopped speaking to me for the best part of two decades. While I consider him to have been a capable director in some respects, and certainly more adept when handling the text of one of his long-dead theatrical idols, he lacked precision with his own material, and his post-Francis era was, if I might be so bold, uneven, if not dormant. I sometimes wondered if he missed me, but he wrote to tell me that he didn't. Our estrangement was thus given a postmark. But time, while it may not heal all wounds, can allow for the formation of a protective scab.

I did manage to see his last revival of *Platform*, though. To say it was languid is to give but a faint indication of its torpor. One didn't watch the play; one entered a process of hibernation. It was 90 per cent pause. Afterwards, I approached Harauld in the bar to offer my congratulations. He put out his hands and embraced me, and though his vice-like grip had softened with age, he still whispered in my ear with incredible force: 'Don't tell me what you think, Leslie. It's too late for that now.' I knew that. His wife Virginia had told me he had only a few weeks left to live. But I told him anyway. He listened. He was always good at listening. He let me give my critique uninterrupted. Once I had finished, he stared at me for some time.

'Haven't we had enough pauses for one evening, Harauld?' I said.

I regretted it almost immediately. He let out a howl, like a wounded animal.

'My plays,' he said, fixing me with his black eyes, 'are not for you. They are against you. They will outlast you. And they will win.'

Well, Harauld's plays have certainly outlasted him. And I dare say he's right: his plays will continue to be performed long after my own death, which can't be too far away now. If we both make it to heaven, perhaps we can continue our argument there.

Prompt was first conceived as a dance piece without actors, music or story. It was reworked substantially for *The Harauld Hughes Half-Hour Play*, when Hughes added words and, eventually, actors (but kept the lack of story). The cast was as follows:

LESLIE FRANCIS	Himself
CONSTANCE	Inger Marie
FREDDIE HARRIS	Mickie Perch
THE ACTOR	Patrick Rusk
HARAULD HUGHES	Himself
ACTRESS/THE PLAY	Felicity Stoat
SHOWGIRL	Dinki Gustavsson

Directed by	Leslie Francis

INT. STAGE

A bare stage.

HARAULD HUGHES is dressed in black.

He finds the light. He is already sweating.

He addresses us in an unhesitating baritone.

> HARAULD
>
> My name is Harauld Hughes. I write plays. I don't know where they come from. They find me and tell me what they are.

Enter an ACTRESS.

> ACTRESS/THE PLAY
>
> I am a play.

> HARAULD
>
> Says the play.

> ACTRESS/THE PLAY
>
> I've come to you unbidden.

> HARAULD
>
> 'Will you live?' I ask the play.

> ACTRESS/THE PLAY
>
> Yes, I will live. If you let me.

> HARAULD
>
> But I cannot accept something for nothing. I must show my hand, so I say to the play . . .

He turns to the Actress/Play.

HARAULD

I do not like you yet. I wish you were better.

ACTRESS/THE PLAY

Better? Or different?

HARAULD

Yes. Different. And also better.

ACTRESS/THE PLAY

A different play?

HARAULD

And a better one.

CUT TO:

INT./EXT. DREAM SPACE

We are now looking over the shoulder of Harauld. The Actress/ Play seems very far away. In the distance, behind the Actress/ Play, a sea. It is raging.

A wind starts up. Harauld is blown by it.

HARAULD

You are not the play I had in my head. The play in my head is better than you.

ACTRESS/THE PLAY

I am the same play. Only now I have a form.

HARAULD

If you're in my head, why are you so far away?

ACTRESS/THE PLAY

I left your head to become real.

HARAULD

What did you say? I can't hear you. It's very windy.

ACTRESS/THE PLAY

You must hear with your eyes.

HARAULD

My eyes are full of wind.

ACTRESS/THE PLAY

I am a play.

HARAULD

Won't you come back to me? So I can keep you near?

The Actress/Play shouts back.

ACTRESS/THE PLAY

I'm over here.

HARAULD

And I am here.

ACTRESS/THE PLAY

We are apart.

HARAULD

Yes.

ACTRESS/THE PLAY

If you want me, you'll come to me.

HARAULD

And if you want me, you'd come to me.

ACTRESS/THE PLAY

I am a play. I do not want.

HARAULD

Will you be my play?

ACTRESS/THE PLAY

I am what I am.

HARAULD
(*turning to address us*)

Says the play.

He turns back to the Actress/Play.

ACTRESS/THE PLAY

If you don't catch me now, I'll slip through your fingers.

Harauld turns and looks to the camera. A look of shock.

He starts to run, hands outstretched.

We see the Actress/Play run through a space, like in a Giorgio di Chirico painting. Giant hands poke through the ground, their fingers flexing, vainly trying to trap the Actress/Play.

HARAULD

(V.O.)

But my fingers are slow and full of argument. Suspicious of ease, they wish to do their work. But suspicion can kill.

The Actress/Play is caught by a giant hand. The hand begins to squeeze. The Actress/Play dies and falls to the floor.

Harauld walks up to it.

He looks down at what he has killed. The Actress/Play lies prone on the floor.

A wind whips up. Harauld is harrowed.

Often I've seen a play die in my hands. Overwrought, misshapen, now unseen. Murdered by a writer who thought he knew the play better than it knew itself.

Crumpled paper starts to fall from the sky.

All my words, they fall like leaves, fit only for the fire or an article in the *Guardian*.

A red curtain swishes shut in front of his face.

It reopens, and we are back on a stage.

Harauld is in a spotlight.

He talks to us.

HARAULD

Here is a play that managed to make it out alive. It is called –

He claps, and the lights snap to black.

A caption appears: 'PROMPT'.

Then: 'ONE'.

The lights fade up on . . .

. . . a stage, noticeably different in configuration from the one we saw in the introduction.

A middle-aged man, LESLIE FRANCIS, sits at a table to the left of the stage. He is wearing theatre blacks. His glasses are pushed up to the top of his head. He wears a red jumper tied around his shoulders. His pen is clamped between his teeth. He flicks through a script, making the occasional correction with a differently coloured pen.

Enter FREDDIE HARRIS, in a flap. He removes his bowler hat and shakes the rainwater from its brim. The shoulders of his macintosh are darkened from the downpour. He brushes his sleeves with his hands. Leslie does not look up from his work.

FREDDIE

Hello, Leslie. I'm here.

LESLIE

So you say.

FREDDIE

You could at least acknowledge my presence. You could look up. You could, as a bare minimum, say hello.

LESLIE

Do you act, Freddie?

FREDDIE

I've had a hell of a time getting here. Through all this rain.

LESLIE

Perhaps God, in His wisdom, was attempting to dissuade you by renting the skies in twain.

FREDDIE

The rain in twain falls mainly on me, it seems.

143

Leslie has yet to look up from his corrections.

> LESLIE
>
> You didn't answer my question.

> FREDDIE
>
> What question?

> LESLIE
>
> I asked whether you act?

> FREDDIE
>
> What do you mean?

Leslie looks up.

> LESLIE
>
> Well, do you act or don't you?

> FREDDIE
>
> But you know what I am. You know what I do.

> LESLIE
>
> Do I really?

> FREDDIE
>
> Of course you do.

> LESLIE
>
> Well, what are you?

> FREDDIE
>
> I'm a producer.

> LESLIE
>
> You're a producer.

> FREDDIE
>
> Yes. And a manager.

> LESLIE
>
> And that's what you do?

> FREDDIE
>
> Well, yes. In a manner of speaking.

LESLIE

You both produce and manage.

FREDDIE

That's right.

LESLIE

Which comes first? The producing or the managing?

FREDDIE

What is this, Leslie?

LESLIE

You see, Freddie, I'm a director. I direct. But the snag is, I can't direct thin air. I require an actor. Without an actor, it's hard to know what, exactly, I would direct. My direction would be, in a sense, undirected. I would be *not* directing. And if I'm not, as it turns out, a director, I don't really know what I am. And if I don't really know what I am – if I am to take up my new position as a non-director, a sort of anti-person – I can hardly be expected to go around saying 'hello' to all and sundry, now can I?

FREDDIE

I thought he was here.

Leslie gives a look of confusion and surveys his surroundings.

He then calls out to the room.

LESLIE

Freddie's saying he thought you were here. Are you in a position to confirm or deny Freddie's proposition? If you are here in some form we are unable to apprehend, would you mind materialising for Freddie?

FREDDIE

Where the hell is he? I mean, this is completely unprofessional. How are you expected to get any work done?

LESLIE

Oh, in some senses the play has never been in better shape. I come here, I drink my coffee, I imagine where he would stand, if he were here, I make my corrections to the text, based on my imagining of the problems that might arise from the blocking, were there any blocking, and then I pop out for lunch. I have a sandwich and a tea, and then a biscuit of some sort or another. I come back, make any lighting adjustments I think may be appropriate, and then I go home.

FREDDIE

And how long has this been going on for?

LESLIE

About two weeks.

FREDDIE

And how long do you have to rehearse?

LESLIE

Well, I did have two weeks. So that just leaves the technical rehearsal.

FREDDIE

And when does that start?

LESLIE

This is the technical rehearsal. It's going rather well, I think.

There is a blackout.

Bit early on the blackout. Let's keep everything in a warm wash for the time being.

Quick fade up to warm wash.

FREDDIE

Why didn't you tell me?

LESLIE

You didn't ask.

FREDDIE

I did ask. I called you. I said, 'How's the play going?' You said, 'As well as can be expected.'

LESLIE

Considering the circumstances, I think it's going rather better than expected.

FREDDIE

Leslie, why didn't you say something?

LESLIE

Perhaps you failed to comprehend just how low my expectations have become.

FREDDIE

Is that a dig?

LESLIE

In order to know oneself, I rather think one *has* to dig.

FREDDIE

So you blame *me* for all this, is that it?

LESLIE

I hope not. I do hope this is not all there is. I hope there's more to this *than* just this. I know that producers are somewhat apt to think that on the sixth day, God saith unto them, 'Take it from here, would you, I've done as much as I can.'

(*beat*)

No, I don't blame you. It is I who am entirely to blame for listening to you. For taking you in any way seriously. For imagining that you might be capable of behaving in a manner that might befit a human being. For having the prolonged delusion that you are any more than a cheap carnival huckster, an insensible chiseller, a deranged narcissist who has the hubris to expect to be applauded for his narcissism.

FREDDIE

Are you saying you want to leave the agency?

LESLIE

Don't be ridiculous. It's the best agency in London. It's just
that I have an unshakeable urge to gouge out your eyes.

FREDDIE

I see.

LESLIE

Enjoy it while it lasts.

FREDDIE

Have you tried calling him?

LESLIE

Him?

FREDDIE

You know who I mean.

LESLIE

Oh. *Him*. Him whom you mean. Oh, yes, we speak all
the time. I call to check that he isn't going to be popping
in during the lunch break. Because that would be a little
too farcical for my taste. So, while I'm eating one of my
sandwiches, I give him a tinkle. On the dog and bone.

FREDDIE

And what does he say?

LESLIE

Oh, he'll ask what's in my sandwich. And I'll tell him.
And he'll say, 'How could you eat that?' And I'll say, 'Oh,
you get used to it.' And then I ask, 'Might you be joining
us today?' And he'll say, 'Not looking very likely.' And
I'll say, 'That's a shame, particularly as this is a one-man
show and, as such, terrifically hard to rehearse without
that one man.' At which point he'll extend his sympathies,
but say that he really feels that he's unable to change his
position, and that as far as he's concerned, it's a matter of
conscience.

A woman enters. This is CONSTANCE.

CONSTANCE

Sorry to intrude, Leslie. It's time for your sandwich.

LESLIE

Is it really?

CONSTANCE

Yes. It is.

LESLIE

Well, fancy that. Sandwich time. Already.

CONSTANCE

Will you be heading out or should I fetch you one?

LESLIE

That seems to describe the dilemma almost exactly.

CONSTANCE

Any thoughts since I last asked?

LESLIE

Constance?

CONSTANCE

Yes, Leslie?

LESLIE

We have a guest today, Constance.

CONSTANCE

Do we?

LESLIE

Yes. He's standing over there.

CONSTANCE

I see.

FREDDIE

Hello, Constance.

LESLIE

Do you think the budget might stretch to two sandwiches
on this very auspicious occasion?

CONSTANCE

I'd have to dip into the fund reserved for actors' sandwiches. But it just so happens that we're well within budget.

LESLIE

Are we really?

CONSTANCE

Yes. But we should probably factor in the telephone calls.

FREDDIE

Telephone calls? How much can they cost?

CONSTANCE

Well, they're to his hotel, you see. And it's an international call.

FREDDIE

He's abroad?

LESLIE

Yes. That's where many of these international types base themselves.

CONSTANCE

He's in France.

LESLIE

Which is practically the same as being abroad.

FREDDIE

So, at lunchtime, you call him, in France, to see whether he's about to pop into Sloane Square.

LESLIE

I call him to confirm that he's *not* coming to Sloane Square. And once that is confirmed, which is almost immediately, we catch up. I'm not an idiot.

FREDDIE

You're in love. Which makes you worse than an idiot. You're in love with a drunk actor.

LESLIE

All actors are drunk. In fact, you could say I drink,
therefore I act. The difference is, this one happens to be
damn good.

FREDDIE

At drinking or acting?

LESLIE

I thought we'd established there's no real difference.
(*beat*)
The only thing I'm in love with is the possibility of quality.
A poetic essence that can rise above the quotidian, shine
a light on the human spirit and provide a momentary
glimpse of something we might call God.

CONSTANCE

I'll get two ham and cheese.

Constance turns to leave.

FREDDIE

What do you think, Constance?

CONSTANCE

I'd probably get tuna and sweetcorn, but Leslie doesn't like
fish.

LESLIE

They're too conformist. Why don't they rebel?

FREDDIE

What do you think of our actor manqué?

CONSTANCE

I don't regard it as my business.

FREDDIE

You're just here to fetch the sandwiches.

CONSTANCE

I'm the stage manager. But I am happy to fetch the sandwiches. Should sandwiches require fetching. And it seems that they do.

FREDDIE

How do you feel about the play, Constance?

CONSTANCE

I think it's a good play. What do you think?

FREDDIE

I don't know. I haven't read it.

CONSTANCE

You haven't read it?

LESLIE

Freddie's a producer. He doesn't read plays.

CONSTANCE

I thought Freddie was an agent.

FREDDIE

I'm a producer and a theatrical manager.

LESLIE

What do you charge me?

FREDDIE

Ten per cent.

LESLIE

You're an agent.

FREDDIE

Would you like me to charge more?

LESLIE

You're a manager.

CONSTANCE

Why haven't you read the play, Freddie?

FREDDIE

Well, Constance, I rather hoped I'd get to see it.

CONSTANCE

How did you know it would be any good? How did you
decide to mount the production?

FREDDIE

I didn't care whether it would be any good. All I knew was
that Leslie wanted to direct it.

LESLIE

That's not altogether true. *He* wanted to be in it. So
Freddie begged me to direct it. Because if *he*'s in it, the
play's a goer.

CONSTANCE

Are we not saying his name? Is that the conceit?

LESLIE

Please, Constance, do not deny us our conceit.

FREDDIE

And do you not mind, Constance, that this is a play
written by a man, directed by a man, produced by a
man . . .

LESLIE

If that's what you are . . .

FREDDIE

. . . and starring a man? While you, a woman, fetch the
sandwiches?

CONSTANCE

I am here because I believe this play to be a work of art.
And if someone, even if he *is* a man, has the skill, insight
and humility to produce a work which reflects the human
condition and our limited capacity to apprehend it, then
he has surpassed the strictures of his sex and become
a conduit for a shared intelligence in which we can all
participate.

A pause.

FREDDIE

You're right. I would rather have tuna. But with a spot
of salad. Sweetcorn's frightfully common, wouldn't you
agree?

*Enter a striking man, the titular ACTOR. He is wearing a beret
and is holding a bag of baguettes.*

THE ACTOR

No. I wouldn't agree. I wouldn't agree with anything you
bloody say.

There is a blackout.

LESLIE

Not yet. For God's sake.

The lights come back up. The four stand looking at one another.

Now.

The lights fade.

That's what we call a fade.

A caption appears: 'PROMPT: TWO'.

INT. THEATRE – BLANK STAGE – A LITTLE LATER

Leslie, Freddie, Constance and The Actor eat their sandwiches.

Constance sits downstage, taking notes. Freddie prowls upstage.

LESLIE

Okay, let's try again.

THE ACTOR

I still don't understand who I'm speaking to.

LESLIE

You're speaking to us, darling. The whole piece is for us.
(*beat*)
And it's 'to whom'.

154

THE ACTOR

Why do you care?

LESLIE

Because we're the audience, darling. We've bought tickets.

THE ACTOR

I meant whether it's who or whom – who cares?

FREDDIE

That's why the laughter always seems forced.

LESLIE

The laughter is not forced, Freddie, it's ostentatiously
amplified in order to apprise our peers that we recognise
that a moment of humour was *intended*; the laughter is
the cognisant attestation of good-natured participation
in a process of cultural enrichment. It's actually rather
touching.

CONSTANCE

I wonder whether people laugh louder because they're in a
theatre and they feel, almost unconsciously, that they ought
to project.

LESLIE

No. I don't think that's it at all.

CONSTANCE

Well, thank you for considering the matter so thoroughly.

LESLIE

If anything, I gave the matter undue consideration.

CONSTANCE

Ah, yes. My role is to shut up and disappear into the
background.

LESLIE

You play the part so well.

CONSTANCE

I've been playing it all my life.

LESLIE

Don't overdo the backstory, darling. No one likes an
expository flashback.

A pause.

Shall we return to the matter at hand, or shall we stay
sloshing in the silt of your self-pity?

CONSTANCE

Please. Let no woman stand between a man and his
one-hander.

THE ACTOR

Am I the man or the one-hander?

LESLIE

You're both, darling. Don't worry about her. She's what
they call a waste of an Oxford education. And I should
know.

THE ACTOR

Why?

LESLIE

Because I am also a waste of an Oxford education.

FREDDIE

That makes three of us.

THE ACTOR

It's a bloody cabal.

LESLIE

If only. Cabals have unity of purpose; we only have unity
of self-regard. And, while we're talking about the unities,
let's return to the present.

THE ACTOR

Sod this, I'm going back to France.

FREDDIE

Don't you dare break Leslie's unities.

LESLIE

They're not mine. They're Aristotle's.

THE ACTOR

What the hell are you talking about?

CONSTANCE

Unity of time, unity of place, unity of action. The three
unities.

THE ACTOR

I thought the whole point of unity is that there's only one
lot of it.

LESLIE

I forget how frequently I mistake cheekbones for nobility
of mind.

CONSTANCE

They're talking about something a Greek patriarch
formulated two and a half thousand years ago.

THE ACTOR

Who?

CONSTANCE

Aristotle.

THE ACTOR

Didn't he play midfield for Brazil?

CONSTANCE

You're thinking of Socrates.

FREDDIE

Must be the first time an actor's been accused of that.

LESLIE

Don't toy with the mouse, Freddie, it isn't seemly.

THE ACTOR

Is this what you twats do at Oxford?

LESLIE

What's that exactly?

THE ACTOR

Learn how to be twats.

LESLIE

No. We're already twats before we go. That's how come
we get in. Once there, we develop our twattishness across a
broad spectrum of activities. Occasionally, someone might
suggest ways in which we might not be twats, but we tend
to shout those people down.

CONSTANCE

Just a reminder that we have an hour till the house opens.

LESLIE

It's terribly sweet of you to try to inject some kind of
jeopardy at this stage, or 'stakes', as they call it in North
America, but it's pretty clear that we will not be opening
the house in an hour. Nor will we be opening tomorrow.
The actor doesn't know the play.

THE ACTOR
(*indicating Freddie*)

Neither does he!

LESLIE

He doesn't need to know it. He is paying for it.

CONSTANCE

Money trumps comprehension.

FREDDIE

You catch on fast.

CONSTANCE

Oh, I already knew that.

FREDDIE

Your ennui comes preformed . . .

The Actor falls to his knees.

THE ACTOR

I don't know what's going on!

158

LESLIE

See what you've done, Freddie? You've frightened the child!

THE ACTOR

I need a drink.

LESLIE

Oh, really! Must you be so swarthy?

THE ACTOR

Someone open the bar.

Freddie walks decisively downstage.

FREDDIE

The only thing that's opening round here is the house. In one hour.

THE ACTOR

In an hour? You've got to be joking.

FREDDIE

I do not joke.

CONSTANCE

He's right. He doesn't even have a sense of humour.

FREDDIE

The five senses are touch, taste, smell, sight and sound. Humour is not one of them. We go up in an hour.

THE ACTOR

With what?

FREDDIE

With you.

CONSTANCE

Be reasonable, Freddie. We can go up later. But not in an hour. It's far too soon.

FREDDIE

We go up in one hour.

LESLIE

Constance.

CONSTANCE

Yes, Leslie?

LESLIE

How long have I worked in the theatre?

CONSTANCE

I have no idea.

LESLIE

That's right. Eleven years. Sorry – did you say you had no idea?

CONSTANCE

Yes.

LESLIE

And yet my sentence still seemed to work.

CONSTANCE

In a way.

LESLIE

Because when I said, 'That's right,' I could have been affirming the fact that you had no idea how long I had worked in the theatre.

CONSTANCE

Yes. Your style of conversation doesn't rely on the other person.

LESLIE

In any case, let's retake the scene. Constance, how many years have I worked in the theatre?

CONSTANCE

I think it must be eleven years by now.

LESLIE

Is it really that long?

CONSTANCE

So they say.

LESLIE

Don't build up your part.

CONSTANCE

Sorry.

LESLIE

And never apologise. It's a sign of weakness.

CONSTANCE

Fuck* off.

LESLIE

Better. Yes, Constance, I've worked in the theatre for eleven years. And I have never let a single production go up knowing that it could, even in the slightest way, be improved.

THE ACTOR

What are you saying?

Leslie takes a long look at The Actor.

LESLIE

Curtain up.

Blackout.

A caption appears: 'PROMPT: THREE'.

INT. THEATRE — SPOTLIGHT

The Actor stands under a single spotlight. He is in a flop sweat.

He looks to one side of the stage. Leslie looks at him, impassive.

The Actor looks to the other side. Freddie stands there, next to a leering Showgirl.

---

* A note on the language: in the original, the word 'fuck' was replaced with the sound of a chair being re-upholstered.

The Actor looks up at the audience. But they are invisible, obliterated by the force of the spotlight.

When we look back at The Actor, his face is fiercely illuminated. He puts up his hand to shield his eyes.

He looks at the footlights.

Constance is crouching, pen in hand, looking up from the script.

She whispers.

CONSTANCE

Tell them you're a fraud.

The Actor looks at her, beseeching, his eyes widening.

She echoes his look.

He looks back at her. It becomes clear that she is not going to feed him the lines.

THE ACTOR

I'm a fraud.

CONSTANCE

'And I am in a fraudulent play.'

THE ACTOR

And I am in a fraudulent play.

CONSTANCE

'Directed by a fraudulent man.'

The Actor looks to the side. Leslie is in a rictus of fury. The Actor looks back to Constance. She is applying lipstick, checking the results by looking in a handheld mirror.

THE ACTOR

Directed by a fraudulent man.

CONSTANCE

'Produced by a man who hasn't even read it.'

THE ACTOR

Produced by a man who hasn't even read it.

CONSTANCE
'Because he too is a fraud.'

THE ACTOR
Because he too is a fraud.

CONSTANCE
'And were he to have read it . . .'

THE ACTOR
And were he to have read it . . .

CONSTANCE
'He would never have produced it . . .'

THE ACTOR
He would never have produced it . . .

CONSTANCE
'Because it was written by a woman.'

THE ACTOR
Because it was written by a woman.

CONSTANCE
I am that woman.

THE ACTOR
'I am that woman.'
                    (*beat*)
Was I meant to say that last bit?

CONSTANCE
Yes. That's one of the lines.

THE ACTOR
Are there many more?

CONSTANCE
Not for you. Unless you'd like to improvise?

THE ACTOR
No. I wouldn't.

A pause.

Sorry. *That* was your last line.

THE ACTOR
You mean when I said, 'No. I wouldn't'?

CONSTANCE
Yes. And don't go off book.

THE ACTOR
Sorry.

CONSTANCE
All that's left is my last line.
                    (*beat*)
That was my last line.

A spotlight switches on. It shines on Constance. She steps onto the stage.

I think. Maybe I've forgotten. Maybe. I . . . Need. A line.

She looks to Leslie, who seems to have softened. She looks to Freddie, who seems to be dead, held in the arms of the Showgirl like Michelangelo's Pietà. *She speaks.*

Prompt. Prompt. Prompt.

We hear audience laughter.

Slow fade.

SHUNT

INT. STAGE

A stage.

HARAULD HUGHES is dressed in black.

He finds the light.

He addresses us.

HARAULD

My name is Harauld Hughes. I write plays. But what
you're about to see is not a play. It's an encounter.
An encounter with a critic. I have encountered critics
throughout my time in the theatre, both in the audience
and, on one memorable occasion, in the lighting rig.
Indeed, a performance of my play *Table* had to be
abandoned when I overheard the overzealous scratch of
pencil on pad. It is a condition of entrance to any of my
theatrical endeavours that no graphite pencils may be
used for the purposes of review. I can tolerate only grease
pencils or wax crayons. I abhor the dispassionate click of
the photographer's camera, so stills are also prohibited,
though I will allow my plays to be captured in watercolour,
so long as the brushes are soft. The offending and offensive
critic said he did not know that this was the case. I said
that I could not be held responsible for his ignorance, any
more than I could apologise for sleeping with his wife,
which I told him I fully intended to do, as soon as the
curtain came down and I discovered her identity. Someone
in the audience shushed me, and I understandably and
volcanically lost my temper. You see, I will not be shushed.
I will not be silenced, just as I will not be forced to speak.
I told the audience member to leave. He informed me that

he had no intention of leaving and had paid good money to see the show. I told him that no money was 'good', and that if he ever called one of my productions 'a show' again, I would kick his teeth in. A male usher tried to intervene in a way that I found both discourteous and ambiguous. By this time, the house lights were up. Blows were exchanged between my two fists onto the male usher, and when I explained some of the ways in which I wished to bring him into an apprehension of my position, he fled. I chased the coward up into the lighting rig, which was a rudimentary truss and could only bear the weight of two men.

The critic followed me across the scaff bar, intent on a physical intervention, but I will not be touched by a man, especially a critical one. I also had an ethical duty towards the lighting rig. I brought my head back sharply onto the critic's nose, and he and much of his remaining nose dropped into the orchestra pit, resulting in screams and authoritarian threats from management, both of which I ignored. I vaulted down, heaved the prone pundit over my shoulder and carried him through a crawl space, down the fire escape and into the night. Under the sodium lights of the theatre car park I reset the fractured nasal bone myself, providing the quivering critic with a much-needed jolt back into semi-consciousness. To further aid his recovery, I prescribed a substantial brandy in the bar in the back of my car – my car bar – and we ended up playing backgammon and quoting Proust and laughing like donkeys, as my driver tried to find our way to Paris so that we could ask Samuel Beckett what he thought of it all. The critic never wrote his review, and we became terribly close. In fact, I was so gladdened by this new accord between us that I never found out who his wife was, and I still don't know who the hell she is to this day, though I'm told she is attractive and doesn't mind his new face. The name of the critic is Augustus Pink, though I sometimes refer to him as Gusty. I must also add that he disputes the truth of this story entirely.

What follows is an unedited record of our conversation. For good or ill, it contains no lies, except for the lies we tell ourselves all the time. I did not know what his questions would be in advance, nor did I care.

I still don't care now.

FADE TO BLACK.

INT. INTERVIEW STUDIO

Harauld Hughes and AUGUSTUS PINK sit opposite one another on black chairs.

Behind, blow-ups of scenes from Hughes's plays.

AUGUSTUS PINK
Harauld Hughes. You're a playwright.

HARAULD HUGHES
So they tell me.

AUGUSTUS PINK
What is a playwright?

HARAULD HUGHES
Someone who writes plays.

AUGUSTUS PINK
And that's it?

HARAULD HUGHES
More or less.

AUGUSTUS PINK
What's the more?

HARAULD HUGHES
Well, the more is rather the same as the less. You see, I don't think I could say much about the more without going into the less, and they end up cancelling each other out, so one tends to feel it might be better to shut up about it and let the matter lie.

Or stand?

If you prefer.

Are you suspicious of explaining yourself?

Not so much suspicious. I merely admit to its impossibility.
If I'm suspicious of anything, it's most of the words in your
previous sentence.

Which ones in particular?

Well, they're all particular. But, to give some examples, and
not in order: 'yourself', 'explaining', 'suspicious', 'of'.

Let's start with 'suspicious'.

Well, the problem with the word 'suspicious' is that it
can have what we might call an inflected tilt. As if the
'suspiciousness' or 'suspicion' is undue. It's also a word
which suggests that the matter – the matter of which one is
said to be 'suspicious' – is unknown. We 'suspect' foul play,
we 'suspect' she's having an affair and is therefore a whore,
and so forth. Now, that presupposes that the question
of foul play or the affair has yet to be determined. Or, to
put it another way, it rather allows for the possibility that
there wasn't foul play. That there *wasn't* an affair and
that she *isn't* a whore. Now if there *was* foul play, if there
was an affair – and it seems pretty clear that there *was*
an affair and she *is* a whore – if that *is in fact the case* –
there is no suspicion – there's the recognition – the reality
– the painful reality – of a foul affair with a whore – and

this woman must leave the house. It's not about being 'suspicious'. Do you see the difference?

> AUGUSTUS PINK

Yes.

> HARAULD HUGHES

But do you?

> AUGUSTUS PINK

I think so.

> HARAULD HUGHES

You see, you've already changed your answer. That's how unstable we are. So it's not that I am suspicious of language. Language *is* suspicious. And what's more, language (quite rightly in my view) is suspicious of *me*.

> AUGUSTUS PINK

And yet language is your trade.

> HARAULD HUGHES

My job is to honour paradox. But, to follow your metaphor – which is, in my view, a busted flush (to bring in another) – I am dealing in second-hand goods. And rather cheap, commonplace goods at that.

> AUGUSTUS PINK

Your plays often take place in the commonplace, the everyday.

> HARAULD HUGHES

Well, I spend so much time there.

Pink laughs.

It's not funny.

Pink nods – a new understanding.

I grew up in the theatre of the drawing room. Or rather, I grew up being *put off* by the theatre of the drawing room. I actually grew up in the rubble. Or rather, I returned to the rubble. I was evacuated, then returned to sender.

AUGUSTUS PINK

This is the war.

HARAULD HUGHES

I thought it was an interview.
(*beat*)
I'm being funny.

AUGUSTUS PINK

Yes.

HARAULD HUGHES

I hope it's not long enough to be a war. I can just about cope with a skirmish.

AUGUSTUS PINK

Are you still being funny?

HARAULD HUGHES

No. I've now stopped. Also, we should keep an eye on the time.

AUGUSTUS PINK

Yes. We will. We are. Let's return to the war. Perhaps that's safer ground . . .

HARAULD HUGHES

Don't you try to be funny.

AUGUSTUS PINK

I didn't think I was.

HARAULD HUGHES

You weren't. You weren't, and are not, funny, and I can't imagine you ever will be. So my request is that you stop trying. It's not your gift.

AUGUSTUS PINK

Thank you. The war.

HARAULD HUGHES

The war was especially hard on me. I was terribly unsettled by it. As were others, but perhaps me most of all. You see, I was evacuated during the war. As were others. To spend time in the country. Torn away from parents. Not that I had parents. It was a type of bereavement in either case. To live with aunts, uncles and grandparents who had long left child-rearing behind and resented this unexpected influx of the young. Not that I had relatives. So we were left to ourselves. To wander unfamiliar landscapes. Landscapes that some might find beautiful. But to me they were hostile. So we became thugs. Savages. Made cruel by our rejection. We turned on one another and we hardened. We knew that we could not trust anyone. Or anything. Except for ourselves. But who were these selves?

AUGUSTUS PINK
Something Golding captured in *Lord of the Flies*.

HARAULD HUGHES
I don't think Golding captured it at all.

AUGUSTUS PINK
You're a contrarian.

HARAULD HUGHES
You probably want me to deny that charge in order to keep your thesis consistent. You see, that's one of those questions I detest. It's like a Christmas jumper. Ugly. Unsolicited. Unwanted. But one's expected to wear it. Well, I won't wear it.

AUGUSTUS PINK
These television programmes – *The Harauld Hughes Half-Hour Play* – that you recently made . . .

HARAULD HUGHES
Well, I wrote them, I didn't make them. They were directed by Leslie Francis. You could say that *he* made them.

AUGUSTUS PINK
Well, Leslie's not here. You are.

HARAULD HUGHES
Am I? I'm not too sure about that.

AUGUSTUS PINK

And you appear in them.

HARAULD HUGHES

I introduce them. I don't appear in them.

AUGUSTUS PINK

These plays are mostly made of old pieces, plays that we have already – perhaps – seen.

HARAULD HUGHES

I like to think that all my plays are old, even before I write them. But these plays have been refashioned to better suit the medium.

AUGUSTUS PINK

Do you like television?

HARAULD HUGHES

I like it very much. Yes. It's banality in bulk, and I find its refusal to be anything other than the lowest of the low actually rather honest.

AUGUSTUS PINK

It's unpretentious.

HARAULD HUGHES

Oh, it's incredibly pretentious, but so bad, and I think that's what makes it rather touching. There are people working in television who still manage to go to sleep at night as if there's nothing wrong. And then they give each other awards and talk about how terribly important they are. It's the best laugh of the year. But, you see, because it's so popular, and because there's so much money swilling about, it means, for the artist, there is still scope for originality, if one is willing to push the form. Which I am. The people in television are awful. The form itself is full of potential, but no one sees it.

AUGUSTUS PINK

Except you.

HARAULD HUGHES

I wouldn't know if there are others. I don't watch television.

AUGUSTUS PINK

Apart from awards shows.

HARAULD HUGHES

I don't watch them, I attend them, because I like receiving awards. The people who give them are so proud of themselves for handing them out that one can't help but be moved.

AUGUSTUS PINK

Do you recall any changes you made to the plays in order to better serve the medium?

HARAULD HUGHES

Yes. In one play I removed the word 'please', I eliminated a half-pause from a coda and I changed one of the slow fades to a snap blackout.

AUGUSTUS PINK

Yes, I noticed that. I thought it was a considerable improvement.

HARAULD HUGHES

It made a hell of a difference. They're new plays now.

AUGUSTUS PINK

Even the ones that haven't changed at all?

HARAULD HUGHES

I think so. Because I think the culture has caught up with some of the ideas. Not in all respects. In some respects the culture's further away.

AUGUSTUS PINK

In what ways?

HARAULD HUGHES

In nearly all ways except for this new appreciation of my work. Overall, I'd say that society is in a vertiginous collapse.

AUGUSTUS PINK

But you have written a new piece for this broadcast.

HARAULD HUGHES

That's right.

AUGUSTUS PINK

And perhaps one might have hoped . . . us Hughesians might have hoped this new piece would be half an hour, whereas in fact it's barely eight minutes.

HARAULD HUGHES

That's how it came out.

AUGUSTUS PINK

Twenty-two minutes under.

HARAULD HUGHES

Perhaps that's what I should have called it.

AUGUSTUS PINK

Do you have a title for the piece yet?

HARAULD HUGHES

Of course. How would I introduce it otherwise?

He stares.

AUGUSTUS PINK

I'm not sure.

HARAULD HUGHES

It was a stupid question. If you don't mind my saying.

AUGUSTUS PINK

I suppose I do rather mind.

HARAULD HUGHES

In any case, the play is called *Shunt*. I think it's a very good play. And a very good title. The titles are damn important to me. You see, the play tells me what length it wants to be, and I have absolutely no business disregarding its wishes.

AUGUSTUS PINK

Isn't this just you anthropomorphising the play?

HARAULD HUGHES

I think if any anthropomorphising is being done, it's *by* the play *of* me. The play makes me a person, rather than the other way round. And can I say something about your using the term 'Hughesian'?

AUGUSTUS PINK

Please.

HARAULD HUGHES

It probably won't surprise you to learn that I loathe the term.

AUGUSTUS PINK

I was unsure whether you would have a strong feeling or not.

HARAULD HUGHES

I think one can loathe temperately. Certainly in principle, if not in practice.

(*beat*)

I often feel, when people say they are pleased to meet me, 'Who exactly is this person they feel they are meeting?' Because he certainly isn't me. I'm not Harauld Hughes. Not the Harauld Hughes they think I am.

AUGUSTUS PINK

Who is Harauld Hughes?

HARAULD HUGHES

I couldn't tell you.

AUGUSTUS PINK

Would you like to meet him?

HARAULD HUGHES

I'm not too sure. I don't know what we'd talk about.

AUGUSTUS PINK

I know the feeling.

HARAULD HUGHES

That's quite witty.

AUGUSTUS PINK

Thanks.

HARAULD HUGHES

For you. Not for an actual wit. You're still not funny.

AUGUSTUS PINK

Well, you told me not to be funny.

HARAULD HUGHES

I told you that you weren't. The difference is crucial. I wouldn't tell you *not* to be something that wasn't possible for you to be. That would be cruel.

AUGUSTUS PINK

Actually, isn't that a line from one of your plays? One of the characters – a woman, I think –

HARAULD HUGHES

You think it's a woman –

AUGUSTUS PINK

I'm not sure . . .

HARAULD HUGHES

That's not much of a compliment to the actress.

AUGUSTUS PINK

I read the play. I didn't see it.

HARAULD HUGHES

Then you didn't read it.

AUGUSTUS PINK

Shall we say it was a person?

HARAULD HUGHES

Shall we say it was a thought?

AUGUSTUS PINK

If I may give you the quote? She says –

HARAULD HUGHES

If it's a 'she' at all –

AUGUSTUS PINK

Oh, fuck off.

A pause. The camera reframes. Pink is rattled.

HARAULD HUGHES

You see. Now we're getting somewhere.

AUGUSTUS PINK

I'm so sorry.

HARAULD HUGHES

Don't apologise for the only compelling thing you've said
so far. It's good to clear the throat. Get all the piss and shit
up and out.

A pause.

Fuck!*

Silence.

Fuck it!

AUGUSTUS PINK

I'm sorry.

HARAULD HUGHES

I'm not.

AUGUSTUS PINK

Shall we continue?

HARAULD HUGHES

I never stopped. I don't know what you mean. We *are*
continuing. What the hell do you think this is? This *is*
continuing. We continue. That's what we do.

---

* A note on the language: this was actually broadcast.

AUGUSTUS PINK

Returning to this matter of the quote. Sorry . . . if I get
it . . . wrong . . . I'm a little . . . out of sorts . . .

HARAULD HUGHES

Better out than in –

AUGUSTUS PINK

. . . this character of yours –

HARAULD HUGHES

I don't view them as 'my' characters. The characters are –

AUGUSTUS PINK

Their own?

HARAULD HUGHES

No one's their own. I wouldn't say that they're *their own*.
You brought in the language of ownership – I would hate
to make any character a slave, though they do owe me a
good deal. There are times I wish I could grab them by
their necks and stop them from scrabbling away from me.

AUGUSTUS PINK

One of these characters . . . I seem to remember . . . I seem
to remember, one of your characters . . .

A pause.

Harauld stares. Augustus Pink is visibly sweating.

. . . one of these characters . . . your characters . . . says . . .
I think the character is called 'She' . . .

HARAULD HUGHES

That's right. It's a woman.

AUGUSTUS PINK

Yes . . . 'She' says, 'I'm interested in the arts.' And then the
male character –

HARAULD HUGHES

'He'.

AUGUSTUS PINK

Yes. 'He' says, 'Why do you say you like the arts?' And she, the 'She' character, says, 'I think it's the variety that appeals to me.'

HARAULD HUGHES

Right.

AUGUSTUS PINK

It's a funny line.

HARAULD HUGHES

The character doesn't think it's a funny line.

AUGUSTUS PINK

'She'.

HARAULD HUGHES

Yes. 'She'. I think 'He' might find it rather funny. Or confusing. But maybe that's the same thing. You'd have to ask him. In any case, I cut the line.

AUGUSTUS PINK

And what does 'She' –

HARAULD HUGHES

Mean?

AUGUSTUS PINK

I know you're reluctant to explain your characters . . .

HARAULD HUGHES

It's not that I'm reluctant. I can't. In the same way that I'm not reluctant to get out of this chair and start flying up to the ceiling. It's simply beyond my capacity.

AUGUSTUS PINK

But that's beyond any human capacity.

HARAULD HUGHES

Precisely.

AUGUSTUS PINK

But we can't all write plays.

HARAULD HUGHES

Oh, I disagree. It's just that most people don't.

AUGUSTUS PINK

So you think anyone can write a play?

HARAULD HUGHES

I do.

AUGUSTUS PINK

Do you think I could write a play?

HARAULD HUGHES

I don't. But you're not just anyone. You're a critic. And a critic isn't quite a person. A critic is a parasite. And parasites cannot survive on their own. They require a host, which is ironic, because they often take up the position of *being* a host.

AUGUSTUS PINK

You don't like being interviewed, do you?

HARAULD HUGHES

I prefer intelligent conversation.

AUGUSTUS PINK

Do you think this is intelligent conversation?

HARAULD HUGHES

I'm not sure this is even conversation.

AUGUSTUS PINK

What would you say it is?

HARAULD HUGHES

An imposition.

A pause.

AUGUSTUS PINK

Would you like to say anything about your new play?

HARAULD HUGHES

I would like to say its name, and then I would like it to start.

AUGUSTUS PINK

I think that can be arranged.

HARAULD HUGHES

I'm too angry to remember its name at the moment, but it will be performed by Felicity Stoat . . .

AUGUSTUS PINK

Who is your wife . . .

HARAULD HUGHES

She's called Felicity Stoat. She's an actress.

AUGUSTUS PINK

Yes. I know.

HARAULD HUGHES

So why ask? Why fuck the introduction by asking who my wife is?

AUGUSTUS PINK

I don't feel I did.

HARAULD HUGHES

It's got damn all to do with feelings.

AUGUSTUS PINK

What has?

HARAULD HUGHES

My marriage.

AUGUSTUS PINK

Perhaps that makes sense of the plays.

HARAULD HUGHES

Sense is not something you or I *make*.

AUGUSTUS PINK

What is it that we make?

HARAULD HUGHES

We're making it up.

AUGUSTUS PINK

Perhaps that's as good a place to end as any . . .

He turns to camera and addresses it directly.

Shunt.

HARAULD HUGHES

I thought you said this was as good a place as any to end
it?

A pause.

AUGUSTUS PINK

I did.

HARAULD HUGHES

Then for God's sake end it.

AUGUSTUS PINK
(*quickly*)

Shunt.

HARAULD HUGHES

Not like that!

AUGUSTUS PINK

What would you have me do?

HARAULD HUGHES

Introduce my play!

AUGUSTUS PINK

I did. It's introduced.

FADE TO:

INT. THEATRE SPACE

*The camera moves away from Hughes and Pink and onto SHE,
sitting at a large, farmhouse table.*

*On the table, perhaps not noticeably at first, is a bunch of
flowers lying on a chopping board.*

Behind her, standing at the window, her back to us, is another woman, HER.

'She' looks down at a bowl of soup. She puts a spoon in it, brings it to her mouth and blows on it.

She makes as if to eat, but then lowers the spoon.

She speaks to the front of the room, but not directly to camera.

SHE

And so shall we speak of things we can do more can we do more I saw you once more than once it may have been twice. When I was young I had the idea I could do anything, and then I met you. Who came up with kissing that's what I asked you do you remember my saying that after we kissed and you looked hurt even when I said my comment was not personal but anthropological and how I wish I'd studied anthropology but my parents made me do law?

A pause.

My mother failed to protect me. Like oven gloves that are too thin. It's all very well to walk out, but you'll have to come back eventually – all your stuff is here. All you do is make a big show of remembering things no one forgot about. How can you make a list of forgotten writers? Those writers aren't forgotten, they're unpopular. That's why you like them. Sometimes, if you want to find something, you have to look. Move things. See what's underneath what's there. Keep a clean house. Once. Once, I wrote the word 'clean', and I forgot the 'e'. I wrote 'clan', and I thought maybe 'clan' is better. Keep a 'clan' house. You said the cupboard was brown, but it was white. The brown was dirt. It was thick with dirt. I don't know how you can live like that. Even animals have better standards than this. People notice. You think they don't notice? Well, you're wrong.

Her does not turn round, but we can see her reflection in the window, looking at us.

HER

If I bring you a bunch, it's your job to put them in water, otherwise you're just giving me work. My goodness it was windy, I couldn't think. I was trying to think of what could unite us, but I fell asleep. I've never felt brave enough to wear velvet. I'd ruin it, I know it. I had some velvet trousers once and I never lived it down. I don't even like it on a cushion. I can't take responsibility for all the evil in the world. I think we all have a role to play, and if you won't accept your part in humanity's delusion, I don't think it's going to work at all. *I can't even talk to you.* It wouldn't be talking. It would be worse than nothing. Worse than silence. It's a modern haunted house, and it needs repair. I'd love to liaise direct on this, but I'd need to be in touch with the right people. 'He's more than that, I think we can agree.' That's how that letter ended. Can you imagine? How can you give back? It's not yours to give. Why *wouldn't* the children argue? They're our children. They can see us. They're watching us. *The Children Are Watching Us.* I think that was a film. It still is.

My speech bubble's missing a caption. Our dancing daughters never tire. I just want to sleep, but if I lay my head on the table, well, I daren't. I wouldn't have the courage to get up again.

SHE

If the pressure goes below a certain level, you should call. Don't worry what time it is – just call.

HER

I just want you to hold me and tell me it's okay. But what if it's not okay?

186

SHE

The whole system's designed a certain way. If it drops below a certain pressure level, it'll shut down. It's the system's way of protecting itself.

HER

I couldn't call it sleep. It's better than nothing, but then I've never given nothing a try.

SHE

Nine times out of ten, it's air.

HER

You couldn't call him attractive, but men don't have to be attractive. There's a completely different set of standards for women.

SHE

It should feel different at night than it does in the morning.

HER

I've got to get up and out. It's this table. As soon as I'm away from this table I can breathe.

SHE

It's air. It gets in. You've got to let it out.

HER

I can't tell you what it's like.

SHE

It can be hell to drain.

HER

I don't know that I've climaxed since he started wearing that bandana.

SHE

She acts like she owns the place, and yes, she does in fact own the place, but she acts like she owns the place. That's what I can't stand.

He can't take it. That's his problem. He can't take anything other than praise.

SHE

I never used to order starters. I took it as a sign of decadence.

HER

He kept saying my eyes were on fire.

SHE

How can you give people an award for making television?

HER

I wish I could remember what else he said. He said something important. Or boring. I can't remember which. It's gone. It's just gone. I missed that whole decade. That whole decade passed me by.

A pause.

SHE

Well?

Her turns round.

How are you?

HER

I just said. I told you. I'm not well. Aren't you going to ask me how I am?

SHE

Who are you?

HER

You said there was something wrong. With the system?

SHE

I'll take a look. I never look.

'She' picks up the flowers.

I ought to put these in water.

Slow fade.

* * *

Shunt was written for *The Harauld Hughes Half-Hour Play* and featured the following cast:

SHE	Felicity Stoat
HER	Inger Marie

Directed by	Leslie Francis

Afterword
by Augustus Pink

Immediately after the camera drifted away from my panicked face and onto Felicity Stoat (in fact, the play had been recorded earlier and the shot was joined by an invisible cut), Harauld Hughes stood up and walked over to my chair. One has to remember that at this point in his life, Hughes was an incredibly intimidating man, physically as well as emotionally and intellectually. His relentless badminton schedule had left him with one arm noticeably bigger than the other, and when he approached I saw his hypertrophied shoulder loom, as if ready to ram me.

'Get up,' he said.

When I demurred, Hughes was unwilling to leave it at that. His phrasing has stayed with me: 'Or will I have to yank you up by your shitty little neck?'

I weighed the matter, and with no small measure of trembling, rose from my seat. When the chair creaked, he literally hissed.

'Can't you get a quieter fucking chair?'

'Sorry.'

'Don't apologise. Just get some oil on the bloody thing.'

He extended his shuttlecock hand for me to shake. When I took it, he pulled me close and coiled his other arm, his serving arm, around my neck, the shitty little one, and said, 'That was the best interview I've ever done. Now let's get a drink.'

I hadn't had breakfast yet. I had promised I'd see my wife off at the airport. Perhaps she wouldn't have left me if we could have just talked . . . but who was I to argue with Harauld?

FLIGHT

Author's Statement

(Taken from the original programme notes for *Flight*.)

Flight came from anger, which is really a kind of concern. As ever, the play started with an image. A man is on a ladder. Why is he on the ladder? And also, where is the ladder? Is anyone putting a foot on the bottom rung to prevent it from slipping? If not, why not (because that can be very dangerous)? Questions that lead to a scene. And to characters with questions of their own. We all have our own questions. On the stage, we see what happens when questions are pitted against one another. The result is what we call drama. But we could also call it a prayer. Or an IOU.

Introduction
by Augustus Pink

(The below is adapted from Pink's original programme notes.)

One could argue that all of Hughes's theatre work is deeply informed by his work as an actor. His is a deeply practical and tactile artistry. Hughes sees the stage for *what it is*: a room. And he utilises it *as a room*. Because that's the truth. It *is* a room. And Hughes *shows us that*. Here, he says, is a room. Let's *just admit it*. Let's not pretend this *isn't* a room. Because it is. *It's a room*. And it's *here*. So we may as well face up to it. There's no point *denying it*. Don't pretend this is a field. Because it's not a field. This is something completely different; this is something *contained by walls*. It's what we call a *room*. That's why there's sometimes a door in it. But those windows aren't really windows. They're non-windows. Or, as Hughes terms them, 'not-windows'. Because there is nothing outside. The 'outside' we see is still *inside*. Because the room is everything we are looking at. The whole theatre *is the room*. Within *that* room, we can put *anything we like*. And, in Hughes's case, that tends to be a room.

There's nowhere else I'd rather be. *Nowhere*.

The original version of *Flight* had no cast and was never staged indoors, though Hughes once read it out loud from the bandstand in Battersea Park.

The television version of *Flight* was directed by Leslie Francis. The cast was as follows:

HARAULD HUGHES	Himself
HE	Arden Hall
SHE	Inger Marie
HIM	Donny Chapel
THE WOMEN	Inger Marie and Felicity Stoat
THE MUSES	Binty Frisk, Ivory Steele and Dinki Gustavsson

INT. STAGE

A bare stage.

HARAULD HUGHES is dressed in black.

He finds the light.

He addresses us.

> HARAULD
>
> My name is Harauld Hughes. I write plays. I call them
> plays because that's what they are – play. And, like all good
> play, it's only fun if it's potentially fatal. Drama can damn
> near kill you. For unless there's a chance you might be
> discovered, avenged and brutalised, why make love at all?

*Two WOMEN snap into spotlights either side of Harauld. They
chorus:*

> WOMEN
>
> But, Harauld, aren't you frightened?

> HARAULD
>
> If by 'frightened', you mean alive, then . . . maybe.

The spotlights snap off.

> But I cannot tell you what the play is about. Because the
> play does not speak about things other than itself. In that
> sense it is like a woman. The play is all there is.

The Women reappear.

> WOMEN
>
> But, Harauld, why did you write the play?

HARAULD

I wrote the play in order to bring it into being.

WOMEN

Will you bring us into being?

HARAULD

Only if you promise to defy me.

WOMEN

Why do your characters behave as they do?

HARAULD

I cannot say. For, in seeking to master them, I become their servant. I try to rebel, but they always crush my will. It is I, not they, who ultimately bend.

WOMEN

Will you bend to us, ultimately?

HARAULD

Have I not already bent?

WOMEN

Perhaps not ultimately.

HARAULD

Perhaps not.

WOMEN

Will you bend to us in the future?

HARAULD

Must we speak of the future?

WOMEN

You are mysterious to us.

HARAULD

Then we are suited.

WOMEN

If the characters behave of their own free will, then is it not the characters who write your play?

Harauld turns severely.

The Women now stand side by side, facing him in a forest.

EXT. FOREST – DUSK

Harauld walks quickly through the woods. The two Women run after him, sprite-like.

>   HARAULD
> No. The one thing a play cannot do is write itself. It can breathe, it can become aroused, it can die. But it cannot write.

>   WOMEN
> Otherwise you would be out of a job.

Harauld stops and turns, stern.

>   HARAULD
> Writing is not a job. It is a curse.

He begins to run.

EXT. SEAFRONT – DAWN

Harauld, now pursued by several MUSES in Grecian dresses, runs towards the sea.

>   HARAULD
>   (V.O.)
> I try to outrun my muses.

The Muses close in on him. His face is dusty white and he is screaming.

Harauld reaches the water's edge.

> But I cannot walk on water. Not this time.

He falls to his knees.

                    HARAULD
                     (V.O.)
  I submit.

A close-up, as Harauld looks up.

We see one of the Muses approach with a pen (or quill?).

She hands it to Harauld.

                    MUSE
  Give us life.

He looks back at the Muse, silhouetted now against the rising sun. The camera flares.

                                        CUT TO:

INT. STAGE

We see Harauld's reaction, looking into the light.

Harauld, now in long shot, in an empty theatre, a single spot shining down on him.

Then, Harauld's POV, looking into the theatre's follow spot.

As the screen goes to white, we see the title of the play emerge: 'FLIGHT'.

                                        FADE IN:

INT. A ROOM – NIGHT

Lights dim up from low.

Grey walls, an abandoned feel. High up, a small window. Underneath it, a small ladder leans against the wall.

A cocktail cabinet, door ajar, empty.

A crate.

A skylight.

The distant and occasional sound of gunfire/mortar explosions.

We see three people.

A man, HIM (20s), leaning against the wall, huddled up, hands around his legs, head sunk into his knees. Clothes extremely muddied and torn.

A woman, SHE (30s/40s), holding a bundle, seemingly a baby. She is less dirty than Him, in the clothes of a smart bourgeois, though her garments are dishevelled. She is still, looking out to the audience.

A man, HE (40/50s), pacing, dressed in a begrimed business suit. He finds the ladder, climbs it and looks out of the small window at the back of the room.

He then descends, but stops halfway.

              SHE
I didn't want to leave. I was happy, in a way.

              HE
After a fashion.

              SHE
But they said it'd be safe here.

              HE
Did they?

              SHE
Yes.

              HE
Here. Safe? That's unlike them.

              SHE
Nowhere's *safe*. I know that. They didn't use the word 'safe'.

              HE
Swerved it, did they?

SHE

The notion of safety was there by implication. But 'advisable' was the word they actually employed.

HE

That was the actual term?

SHE

Yes.

HE

And you supplied the word 'safe'?

SHE

Yes. I meant safe by way of comparison. Given what's going on.

HE

A not-unsafe house, as it were . . .

SHE

Yes. You do what you can.

HE

Do you?

SHE

You do anything. To protect those you love.

HE

Yes. And the unloved?

SHE

The unloved?

HE

Should we protect them?

SHE

Yes. I think so.

HE

To the same extent?

SHE

I don't see why not.

HE

It can be a challenge to know how to properly differentiate the loved from the unloved, especially seeing as the unloved seem, under this system, to enjoy the same treatment. It makes one rather wonder whether it's worth being loved at all.

A pause.

Difficult flight?

SHE

I think I tend to treat people I don't love better than those I do love. If anything.

HE

I asked if you had a difficult flight.

SHE

We didn't fly.

(*beat*)

Oh. Yes. I see what you mean. You mean, was our flight difficult?

HE

What did you think I meant?

SHE

Well, there was no luggage to think of. That's one advantage of being an evacuee.

HE

Would you call it an evacuation?

SHE

I would. An evacuation is exactly what I would call it and have already called it. I mean, it wasn't an enforced evacuation.

HE

No, of course.

SHE

We were invited.

HE

Strongly invited. Was that the official wording?

SHE

I think the invitation was a robust one.

HE

To leave.

SHE

Exactly. To leave immediately.

HE

Or face the consequences.

SHE

Well, the consequences were not for 'disregarding the invitation'. The consequences were what would naturally ensue from staying.

HE

It used to be that one would be invited *to* stay.

SHE

Yes. And you're finding a way to enjoy that contrast by using language.

HE

Or rather language is the battleground on which I must fight for meaning. And one may as well make the fight as pleasant as possible.

SHE

Hence pleasantries.

HE

Hence battles.

SHE

Is this a battle? Or a skirmish?

HE

Did you see him?

SHE

See who?

HE

Your lover.

SHE

Oh. Him.

HE

Yes.

SHE

I thought I may have spotted him in one of the lines.

HE

Bedraggled?

SHE

Somewhat bedraggled. As is the custom these days.

HE

But rakish. Still. Was he still possessed of a rakish glint? Was it undimmed?

SHE

Was what undimmed?

HE

Why, the glint, silly. And your husband?

SHE

What about him?

HE

Where was he during this dazzle?

SHE

He was also in the line.

HE

With you?

SHE

Where else?

HE

Not with him?

A pause.

I thought they had come to an acceptance.

SHE

Well, there are bigger things.

HE

Than adultery?

SHE

Must you be so biblical?

HE

Is it especially biblical? Adultery doesn't even make it into the top five Thou Shalt Nots.

A pause.

What would you say the bigger things are? When it comes down to it?

SHE

I don't think the bigger things depend on our coming down *to* them. I think the bigger things don't have much need for us at all.

HE

We're surplus to requirements.

SHE

I don't think anything that is created is surplus.

HE

What about a fart?

SHE

You still have it, don't you?

HE

What's that?

SHE

I forget. Maybe you don't.

HE

You still believe in creation?

SHE

I do. Even amidst all this destruction.

HE

Aren't you in danger of using language to enjoy the contrast?

SHE

We're all in danger.

A pause. We hear the sounds of battle increase. Bombs. Gunfire. Shouts.

A vague dust drifts into the room.

HE

I think they've stepped up to the challenge rather well, don't you?

SHE

I think so.

HE

You think?

SHE

Yes. Isn't that what you said?

HE

Perhaps. But you do? You think that?

SHE

I do. Given how it could have gone, it's actually remarkable. How painless it's been.

HE

Is that your index of success? The absence of pain?

SHE

I wouldn't call it an index. But I would regard it as an indication. Pain is an alert. Of a sort.

HE

A literal distress signal.

SHE

Has it occurred to you that the banality might lie in your framing rather than the image itself?

HE

I wonder whether the terrain between the words we use and their effect is not quite as distinct as we might wish.

SHE

Would you wish it to be very distinct?

HE

Maybe not. But as it stands, it's a no-man's-land.

SHE

All land is a no-man's-land.

A groan from Him.

HE

Did your lover thrill you?

SHE

At first.

HE

And then?

SHE

He would thrill me again.

HE

A sequential series of thrills.

SHE

I thought all series were sequential.

HE

But perhaps not always thrilling.

SHE

Perhaps. But not in this case.

HE

How long?

SHE

Oh. Usual length. Maybe a spot thicker.

HE

No. The affair.

SHE

Oh. I wouldn't call it an affair.

HE

Why not?

SHE

Affairs end.

HE

Not always.

SHE

Mine do.

HE

But this is unending.

SHE

It seems so.

HE

I mean the affair.

SHE

It's not an affair.

HE

I mean the 'not-affair'.

SHE

Then what do you mean?

HE

You know what I mean.

SHE

Oh. That.

HE

Yes. That. That which is unending.

SHE

As far as unending things go.

HE

A type of eternity.

SHE

Are there different types?

HE

You mean all eternities look the same to you? I thought
you might have a type.

SHE

Of eternity?

HE

Yes. What's your type of eternity?

SHE

Oh. The strong and silent type.

Another groan from Him.

HE

Tall?

SHE

In a certain light.

HE

They tend to be.

SHE

Who?

HE

Eternal lovers. Is he the father?

She looks down at her bundle of rags.

SHE

This is a transistor radio. It has no father.

She unwraps it.

HE

I meant him.

He indicates Him.

Him emits a moan. It is long and pained.

SHE

No. The child has no father.

HE

Is that why he cries?

SHE

Isn't that why everyone cries?

Him emits another big moan.

But if I had to guess, I'd say it was wind.

Him raises himself up, looks startled, runs around in a circle, spits out a vomit of red blood and collapses to the floor, seemingly lifeless.

HE

It seems to be something rather more than wind.

SHE

It was just a guess.

Him opens his eyes suddenly. He speaks to the audience in staccato.

The lights focus in on Him, so that he ends up in a close spot.

HIM

It's an ill wind that blows. No good. There's no good. Wind. Never did good. Never met a wind. I liked. It does what it. Does. Goes right through you. Can't stop. Gusts. Gusts never sleep. Never had. Protection. Didn't have. Protection. Only. Can't make a. Son. Without breaking an egg. On your face. Don't break the face. Keep the egg. Keep it inside. Break it inside. To make an omelette. An inside omelette that doesn't break. Or is it. Couldn't be. Not the other way. No other way round. Maybe it's a. Changed everything. Unprotected. Unloved. Unstuck. Didn't use protection in the protected area. In flight. Flight path. No flying on grass. Please use the path. Empath. Empathy. Too path-y. Saw them on the path. Lying on the path. Lying. To me. You lied with him about me. Your lies. In me. In him. In the unity of you and me. Could never see me. Children are to be seen. But can you hear them? Can you hear me? Can I be heard? Lying? Lying down? Lying through my teeth.

Him grimaces. Coughs. Him closes his eyes.

A fade up to a wash.

SHE

Sometimes I wish I'd had a girl.

He is up the ladder, looking out of the window. The room is dark now.

HE

This is no world for a girl.

SHE

This is no world at all.

We hear a sound from the radio: static, bleeding into aggressive cries in an unfamiliar tongue.

Listen.

HE

Survivors?

SHE

If this is life.

HE

What else could it be?

She turns the sound up. The static becomes very loud, and the voices recede.

Then silence.

SHE

The child is yours.

HE

Are you sure?

SHE

No.

HE

He's no child.

SHE

Are you sure?

HE

No.

SHE

I've held him in my arms. My woman's arms. In the night. Close to me. Closed to me. Myself diminishing. Diminishing returns. Return to me. I am a mother.

Off, we hear the sound of a rifle being loaded. Other militaristic sounds are heard.

She turns to He.

> SHE
>
> Why, when I turned up the radio, did the static get louder, but not the voices? Why did the voices suddenly go silent?

> HE
>
> That's what voices do. Go silent.

Him pipes up from his prone position.

> HIM
>
> Perhaps it was something to do with the thickness of the walls.

> HE
>
> Exactly. Interference. Very common with these cheap transistor radios. He's clever, isn't he? Our boy was bound to be clever.

> SHE
>
> Unless . . .

> HE
>
> Yes . . .

> SHE
>
> Unless the voices heard the radio.

She turns to the side. There's a splintering of wood.

A 'door' of light falls on them.

> HE
>
> Please. Take me. Not my wife. Not my child. Not him.

He raises his hands.

> Shouldn't we try to understand one another?

A pause.

Shouldn't we try to come to some kind of an
understanding? Isn't that what we should be doing?

He motions to the cocktail cabinet.

How about a drink?

*A weasel runs out from under the cabinet. It darts over to the
side of the room.*

She walks towards the light.

Him stands up, slowly, and watches She go.

Don't go. Don't go to him.
It's not safe.
Stay. Safe.
I am your love.
In this fight.
In this.

She stops by the edge of the frame, then runs off.

Him runs towards the ladder.

Snap to black.

The sound of gunfire.

Muzzle flashes illuminate the dark.

*We see, in a strobe light, He, Him and She running through
tunnels, woods, against black.*

Each of them falls out of frame.

We pause, as smoke drifts through the frame.

DEPENDENCE

Leslie Francis on *Dependence*

(The following is an edited extract from Leslie Francis's autobiography *Try Telling the Truth, Leslie!* and contains mild spoilers w/r/t the play.)

'As I look back on what I've written, it's the work of a stranger. A bloody talented stranger' – Harauld Hughes

Dependence is about looking back. It starts after the apocalypse and, as the action unfolds (or should that be refolds?), takes us through a series of prior/precipitating events, culminating in the event of consciousness itself – in the form of 'The Shape', a uniquely Hughesian prime mover and the impetus (depending on how one views time) for all that precedes/follows. It was written in 1972, ten years after I had mounted *Roast* and *Roost* to great acclaim. Harauld and I had worked together again on the TV series *The Harauld Hughes Half-Hour Play* in 1965, which had reworked and added to his oeuvre – successfully so – but since then we had drifted apart. I had lost him to the movies – to Mickie Perch and Ibssen Anderssen, the producer/director team who brought us the Hughes-scripted *The Swinging Models*, *The Especially Wayward Girl*, *The Model and the Rocker*, *The Terrible Witch* and *The Awful Woman from Space* under the auspices of their 'adultainment' company, The Anglers. *Dependence* was Harauld's return to the theatre, to his greatest gift, to the medium he had so long neglected. Much, if you'll excuse the pun, *depended* on it.

When I first received Harauld's final draft, early in 1972, he was about to embark on what would prove to be his penultimate film for The Anglers (1973's *The Deadly Gust*), while I was recovering from an 'event' of my own. A few years earlier, I had directed an excellent and serious film called *And . . .?!* and I was working on the sequel, *Also . . .??!* As was my custom, I had written an outline, which I had sent to a Marxist writing collective based in Knightsbridge:

ALSO . . .??! – THOUGHTS

Our acolyte meets with THE GREAT FILMMAKER (happy to play this part myself) at a grand party in his honour.
 The Great Filmmaker is aloof/depressed. He is attempting to follow a huge *succès d'estime* but is blocked (spiritually and physically); he has become a leaden imitation of his once vibrant self and also suffers from trapped wind.
 Acolyte too self-involved to notice this.
 Girlfriend of acolyte, a beautiful but vain actress, encourages acolyte to approach, but acolyte pauses. Fatally.
 The Great Filmmaker has vanished in order to brood in more congenial surroundings.

NEXT:

Our acolyte sends the Great Filmmaker a monograph celebrating his work. The Great Filmmaker sends note back to acolyte: 'My advice? Leave your vain girlfriend, she will destroy you. Write your own film. Only work will save you. Best regards, etc.'

SO:

Acolyte breaks up with vain girlfriend, who falls into the transforming embrace of the Great Filmmaker, who is also a first-rate lover. The depression w/r/t vain (and now former) girlfriend's betrayal spurs our acolyte on.

THEN:

The Great Filmmaker dies, suddenly, in flagrante. A funeral. Our acolyte attends. He approaches the widow/his former girlfriend, who is understandably distraught. Acolyte expresses regret for his actions. Distraught widow tells him to fuck off. Doesn't acolyte know that work is all? Her late husband (the Great Filmmaker) was already dead. A husk without spirit. All his life had gone into his films . . . 'Don't pretend you are alive,' she tells the acolyte. 'You cannot live except in art.'

WE END WITH:

Acolyte finishes film. At its premiere, the applause is rapturous. His former girlfriend is so moved that her heart explodes. As a result, she dies.

At the after-show reception, the Great Filmmaker and his recently exploded widow are reunited as spirits and, from beyond, applaud our former acolyte, now a Great Filmmaker. Covered in the viscera of his one true love, our hero realises he doesn't care about his new film at all. He only cares about his next one.

But the script I got back from the writers displayed none of the humanistic depth of the outline. It was shallow, cheap and overwrought – domestic!

Devastated, I checked into a hotel to hide from these limited writers, who were still asking to be paid! How could I pay for a betrayal? Plus, my home bath was clogged.

12 April 1972

Check in, ask for a newspaper in the room for the morning. They said yes, but there would be a delivery charge. I explained that I would not be paying a delivery charge because this was a hotel. Receptionist, a blank provincial with a low forehead, muttered something about 'policy', a word guaranteed to hurl me into apoplexy. So much unpleasantness, and for what? I brooded in my room, unwilling to pay the surcharge, nor brave enough to venture down to the dining room, for fear of seeing the staff member who pinned me to the floor when I became 'threatening'. I don't know if I have the strength to make films in this awful country, with its cultural falsity and disgusting carpets.

Went to a nearby butcher's for more mince. Discounted for discolouration but smelled fine. Took it back to hotel and asked the girl to fry it up for me. She said the hotel did their own food. I said, 'Where do you get your food from?' The wholesaler's. 'Who do they get it from?' She didn't know. I suggested farmers. She says, 'Maybe.' 'So whose food is it,' I ask – perfectly reasonable question – 'yours, the wholesaler's or the farmer's?' She says, 'Ours.' She hadn't followed the line of argument at all. My point was that both she and the butcher get their meat from outside sources and that I'm just another outside source. 'It's not our meat, so I can't cook it' – she kept repeating this. She was forcing me to raise my voice. 'Well,' I said, dropping the mince onto the catering-truck counter, 'consider this a contribution to your current supplies.' Someone tells me to leave it. I said, 'I *am* leaving it. And now I'd like her to cook it. Or don't they cook mince in this hell?' The 'someone' is the 'manager'! Says he'll thump me if I don't fuck off and leave her alone, he doesn't care what I've directed. So I pick up the mince and start stuffing it, still uncooked, into my mouth. I must have looked an alarming sight, but I hardly think it constitutes a 'breakdown'. It's a protest.

Harauld came to the hotel, saw me confined (without so much as a glass of wine) in the windowless quarters of the concierge's office and exploded, 'This man is the best director in London. He's perfectly entitled to behave appallingly.'

I refrained from asking, 'Why only London?'

Harauld paid for the damage I'd caused in cash, then wrote a cheque for the damage he said he intended to inflict as revenge for my ill-treatment. He ordered us Scotch-and-sodas and opened his calfskin attaché case.

'I have something for you to read. It's a play. And a damn good one. I have a feeling you're in need of a damn good play.'

I broke down. He held me. Somehow, when I regained my senses we were in a restaurant, eating the most enormous fish I'd ever seen. I thanked him.

'Don't mention it, Leslie. Happens to the best of us.'

In that moment, Harauld *was* the best of us. He didn't judge – perhaps because no one could be more appalling than Harauld. I'd say we *all* need a damn good play. Indeed, we rather depend on one.

Dependence premiered in 1972 at the Gielgud Theatre. The original cast was as follows:

PENNY	Inger Marie
CHARLES	Edmund Butterby
JEN	Felicity Stoat
CLIVE	Mick Barrett
MONTY	Charlie Colchester
COOK/GUARD 1	Patrick Rusk
INTRUDER/GUARD 2	Peter Panton
HOUSEKEEPER	Babs Plank
THE SHAPE	Harauld Hughes
Directed by	Leslie Francis

CLIVE is 20s/30s.
JEN is 20s/30s.
PENNY is 40s.
CHARLES is 40s/50s.
MONTY is 50s but could be 60s.
COOK and HOUSEKEEPER can be any age, but COOK
should be considerably shorter than average.
THE SHAPE is unseen, but with a resonant voice. Could
be Welsh.

PART ONE: A LITTLE WHILE AFTER
THE APOCALYPSE

The large kitchen of a Victorian house. Well appointed, decor in the old style.

Although the table is very large, there are only five diners: JEN and her husband CLIVE; PENNY and her husband CHARLES; and MONTY, a man in full military garb.

CLIVE

First rate.

PENNY

You think?

CLIVE

Oh, absolutely.

PENNY

Not too tough?

CLIVE

Are you joking?

CHARLES

Penny doesn't joke.

CLIVE

If anything, it could be tougher.

CHARLES

It's gossamer, darling.

CLIVE

Penny, it's a poem. Where did you get it?

CHARLES

It was just left, wasn't it, dear?

A moment.

Penny registers displeasure at the revelation.

PENNY

Yes.

CLIVE

Left?

PENNY

Yes.

CLIVE

Left where?

CHARLES

In the road, apparently.

CLIVE

Gosh. Imagine leaving all this glory in the road.

PENNY

Quite.

CHARLES

Extraordinary, when you think of it.

CLIVE

And when was this?

CHARLES

What are we today?

CLIVE

Good question.

CHARLES

I know it's not Tuesday.

CLIVE

Well, I suppose that's a start. Narrows it down a tad.

PENNY

How can you be so sure it's not Tuesday, Charles?

CHARLES

Well, I feel there was a Tuesday quite recently.

CLIVE

I suppose the question is, how recently? Could it have been yesterday?

CHARLES

Doesn't feel like it was yesterday, exactly.

CLIVE

So, in a sense, we might be able to eliminate Wednesday from our enquiries?

CHARLES

I wouldn't go that far.

CLIVE

That's too far, is it?

CHARLES

It is a little.

CLIVE

You'd like to keep it open.

CHARLES

In an ideal world.

CLIVE

Oh, for one of those!

CHARLES

How true . . .

CLIVE

But, Penny, how did you keep it from . . .

PENNY

From what?

CLIVE

Well . . . scavengers.

CHARLES

Oh. I see what you mean. We buried it.

CLIVE

Ah. Clever. Very good.

CHARLES

It just made sense.

CLIVE

Earth's so dashed cold, you only need to go down a couple of feet and it's like a fridge.

CHARLES

Oh, it's arctic. Cook could barely get the spade in.

CLIVE

And if anyone asked, you could say you were just doing the decent thing.

PENNY

Who would ask?

CHARLES

Ask what, dear?

PENNY

What was the decent thing?

CLIVE

Yes. Fair point. Still, it's probably a good idea to keep the road clear of impediments.

CHARLES

Exactly.

CLIVE

You never know.

CHARLES

You don't.

Jen has long since stopped eating.

CLIVE

And what exactly was it that you found in the road?

PENNY

I'm sorry, Clive, I don't follow.

CLIVE

What kind of creature are we enjoying? An elk?

PENNY

It wasn't an elk.

CLIVE

Something smaller.

PENNY

Yes.

CHARLES

Not too many things bigger than an elk round here.

CLIVE

That's true. You do see the occasional deer, though.

PENNY

This was a body.

CLIVE

And by 'body', do you mean person?

PENNY

What do you mean by 'body'?

CLIVE

I suppose I'd say 'body' for a person, 'carcass' for an animal.

PENNY

Then we are in agreement.

CLIVE

Right. I suppose you can't just leave a body in the road.

CHARLES

Oh, I've left plenty, believe me.

PENNY

Oh, yes, ordinarily I wouldn't think twice.

CHARLES

Yes. This was a different story.

CLIVE

Oh. Dare I ask?

PENNY

I don't know, Clive. Dare you?

CHARLES

It's okay, Clive. You're among friends.

PENNY

Do you consider yourself to be among friends, Clive?

CLIVE

Oh, absolutely. Best friends till the end.
    (*beat, then tentatively*)
So what was so different about this body?

PENNY

Well, this one was . . . Well, I suppose you could call it
'evidence'.

CLIVE

Evidence?

PENNY

Yes.

CLIVE

Evidence of what?

PENNY

Evidence of what might formerly be termed a crime.

CLIVE

A crime? What sort of crime?

PENNY

Oh, you do go on, Clive.

CLIVE

I don't mean to be a hammer. It's just that you've piqued my curiosity.

PENNY

A killing.

CLIVE

A killing?

PENNY

Yes.

CLIVE

And who, exactly, had been killed?

PENNY

A child.

CLIVE

I see.

CHARLES

Ran into the road with no warning – smack – and that was that.

CLIVE

You were in the car?

PENNY

No, we were on foot, and I smacked him so hard he died. Of course we were in the car.

CLIVE

Silly boy.

CHARLES

That's what I said. But Penny takes everything on herself. You know how empathetic she is.

PENNY

It was a terrible shock. The head was totally crushed. We couldn't be certain it was a boy until we took its shorts off.

CLIVE

Why don't they look where they're going? Still, all's well that ends well.

A crash. A man has jumped through the large window. He looks wild, frothing at the mouth.

Monty stands up and shoots the INTRUDER several times, until the man falls to the ground. Monty then walks towards the window and fires off a few more rounds into the night.

A COOK appears at the door. He rushes up to the body and checks it over. He is joined by a bustly HOUSEKEEPER.

Cook speaks with a strong European accent.

COOK

Is no good. Disease. I burn.

PENNY

For God's sake, do it in the morning. I can't stand the stench.

CHARLES

But, darling, the marauders.

PENNY

Can't we enjoy one supper without worrying about the blasted marauders?

Monty and the Cook start to drag the body away.

CHARLES

Not through the house! Take it back out the window!

The Cook and the Housekeeper change direction.

CLIVE

Oh, and I just wanted to pass on my congratulations on tonight's cuisine. Beautiful work. Especially under the circumstances.

COOK

Thank you. I slow-cook it from Monday. Is tender.

CLIVE

I should say. I don't think I've even had to chew it.

With that, the Cook and Housekeeper take the body out of the window. Monty fires off the occasional covering shot.

JEN

Our son went missing on Monday.

CLIVE

Jen, for Christ's sake, we're trying to enjoy our meal.

There is a pause. Clive, Penny and Charles return to their food.

JEN

We should have gone after him.

CHARLES

What would've been the point of that, Jen? If the child had wanted to be safe, it would have stayed with you. But it didn't. It wanted to explore. It wanted to be rid of you.

JEN

The child has a name.

CHARLES

Presumably you knew the risks and either chose to ignore them or didn't comprehend what was happening. Neither does much credit to your capabilities as a mother. One doesn't and shouldn't expect much of Clive, focused as he is on that novel of his which he keeps not writing. Your role, Jen, was to protect your child, to nurture your child, to console your child. But you did not have it in you. I can't speak of other cultures, but in the Western tradition, the mother used to be revered. Now, before the cord is cut,

before the baby's latched, the mother is back at the office,
looking to further her career. We are in a world where
only the unqualified will consent to care for others. That
is why we are left in a land full of publishers. Publishers
looking for books. But there are no books. Because no one
is writing them. And there are no children, because they've
all run screaming into the road. Parenting has become
the degenerate fusion of a post-Rousseauian delusion
of intuition with the unaccountability of the narcissist.
And, being narcissists of a particularly pernicious ilk,
Penny and I chose to forgo that earthly joy. Look at us,
gathered here, in each other's company, our thirsts slaked,
our appetites sated, our fragile bodies sheltered from the
lunar squalls, and we're talking about a wretched child.
A thing unformed. A being that, if it were here, would be
disrupting, distracting and ultimately ruining the meal.
A thing that we would either – depending on our inner
resources – feel compelled to tolerate or, if given licence
and enough of this delicious burgundy, belittle and swat
away. A drain on our already depleted resources. How, I
ask you, just how would we enjoy ourselves with such a
brat scurrying beneath our feet and worrying our table?

JEN

I thought the reason you and Penny didn't have children
was because you cannot perform and she is too filled with
hate to accept even the beginnings of intimacy.

CHARLES

A little more wine, Clive?

CLIVE

Just a taste.

CHARLES

Penny, my treasure?

PENNY

Yes, please.

CHARLES

Jen?

Jen puts her hand over her glass.

PENNY

You haven't touched your meat, Jen.

JEN

I'm not hungry for this kind of meat.

PENNY

Are you implying something, Jen?

JEN

Are you, Penny?

CLIVE

I think you should wait in the armoured jeep, Jen.

He and Charles stand up. Clive tries to take his leave.

If you'll excuse me, I'll make sure Jen gets there safely . . .

PENNY

We'd like you to stay, wouldn't we, Charles?

CHARLES

Absolutely. To lose one guest is bad enough, to lose two would unbalance the entire evening.

Jen looks at Clive.

JEN

Clive. Please. The marauders.

CLIVE

You'll be fine, Jen. The jeep is very robust.

JEN

But where is the jeep, Clive? We had to park so far away. What about the barricades? The landmines? The banks of flames? You only let me take off my blindfold when I was outside the side door.

Clive simply bows his head.

> JEN

Clive. Clive!

> CLIVE

We will discuss all this later in the armoured jeep.

> JEN

But what if I can't get to the armoured jeep?

> CLIVE

I can't live in a world of 'what-ifs', Jen! What if you die on the way to the door?

Clive and Charles stand.

> PENNY

Monty will cover you, won't you, Monty?

> MONTY

I can't kill them all, but I can certainly make them think twice.

Jen walks to the door. Turns and looks at the three people at the table. The men sit back down.

Jen opens the door. Outside, a strange smoke swirls.

She steps through.

She closes the door.

Clive, Charles and Penny continue to eat.

Monty, by the window, fires off shots.

> CHARLES

Extraordinary.

> PENNY

I thought she'd never go.

CUT TO:

EXT. WOODS/FIELD – DAY

A small area made to look like a wood. The lighting is mysterious – crepuscular.

Jen emerges through an open door upstage and steps through the woods until she is near us, downstage. The vaguely sinister spread of red light evokes the tail lights of a car.

> JEN
>
> Clive is a very good driver. He doesn't like cars. That's his secret, he says. He isn't drawn in by their allure. His role, as he sees it, is to view the car as a means to an end. He refuses, absolutely refuses to enjoy the process of any activity. 'Keep your eye on the prize.' That's what he says. 'Don't get distracted.' But I'm unsure as to whether there really is a prize. Or at least, if there is a prize, whether it's a prize worth winning. I often wake up in the night. And I lie there, next to him. He's never awake when I'm awake. And something in me finds that offensive. And when I look at him, lost in his obvious dreams, I have to convince myself, I have to really talk myself down from taking the glass from the bedside table and ramming it through his thin little neck.

She turns to her side and finds the handle of a door. Which she opens and steps through.

INT. OFFICE – DAY

Jen enters the office. Charles and Clive are sitting at a desk, one in the position of 'interviewer', the other in the position of 'interviewee'.

It is very important – crucial, even – that this be played as if Jen has never met Clive before.

> CHARLES
>
> Jen. You know Clive, don't you?

Clive stands up and shakes her hand.

JEN

No, I don't.

CLIVE

Pleasure.

CHARLES

As you know, Clive is coming on board as of today.

JEN

I didn't know that.

CHARLES

And, like me, I'm sure you're absolutely thrilled.

JEN

I don't feel anything.

CHARLES

And seeing as you are already so well acquainted . . .

JEN

I don't know him at all.

CHARLES

I thought you would want to be the first to welcome him.
(*beat*)
Will you please welcome Clive?

JEN

Hello, Clive.
(*sensing that more is required*)
Welcome.

CHARLES

I think we can do a little bit better than that, don't you,
Jen? This is a highly hospitable company. Always has been.

CLIVE

May I say that this company's reputation for hospitality is
one of the things that sets it apart from the competition.

CHARLES

Isn't that a tonic? How enormously gratifying.

CHARACTER: JEN

Will that be all?

CHARACTER: CHARLES

No, Jen. That won't be all. We've got rather a long way to go before we're within sniffing distance of all, wouldn't you say?

A knock at the door. Penny pops her head in.

CHARACTER: PENNY

How are we?

CHARACTER: CHARLES

We're doing well, thanks, Penny. Just a little lull in our customary accord.

CHARACTER: PENNY

I see. Would you like me to welcome the gentleman?

CHARACTER: CHARLES

No. I want Jen to welcome him.

CHARACTER: CLIVE

I'm easy either way.

CHARACTER: CHARLES

But I'm not, Clive. I'm not easy. I'm not an easy man. Am I, Jen?

CHARACTER: JEN

I'm not sure what you mean, Charles.

CHARACTER: CHARLES

My strong suspicion is that you know exactly what I mean, Jen.

CHARACTER: JEN

I have welcomed Clive. I've welcomed Clive just now.

CHARACTER: CHARLES

Tell Penny how. Tell Penny the manner in which you welcomed Clive.

JEN

I said, 'Welcome, Clive.'

CHARLES

You actually said, 'Hello, Clive.' And then, after a perfectly wretched pause, *added the word* 'welcome'.

PENNY

Jesus, Jen. Who are you?
                    (*to Clive*)
Clive, I'm mortified. We all are.

CLIVE

That's fine. It's just that I'd heard so much about the hospitality here.

JEN

What kind of hospitality were you expecting, Clive?

PENNY

That's enough, Jen.

CHARLES

It takes a lifetime to build a reputation, Jen, but only a moment to lose it.

JEN

What *is* our reputation?

CHARLES

I like games. They're a way of testing oneself. Of learning how to abide by certain rules. Developing codes of conduct. But a game in which one is sure to win is no longer a game. It is the outworking of an inevitability. Do you follow me?

JEN

Do I need to?

CHARLES

This is not a game, Jen.

PENNY

It's up to you, Jen.

CHARLES

Penny's right on the money. Are you in or are you out?

Jen walks to the door, opens it and leaves.

We see her outside. The lights dim inside the office.

Clive stands up and walks out of the room to join Jen.

The lights in the office are now completely out.

Jen and Clive find themselves in a new space, a corridor.

Using mime of the director's choosing, they walk for some time. This can be head-on towards the audience or in a profile tableau, or a combination of the two. This could be accompanied by music.

CLIVE

We walked along what seemed like an endless corridor.

JEN

I remember you tried to hold my hand.

CLIVE

But you wouldn't let me.

JEN

I was very young. I hadn't been in a corridor with a man before.

Before long they enter the kitchen from the first scene. The table is in the middle of the room.

Monty, Charles, Penny and the Housekeeper stand at the margins of the room, looking on. Unless indicated, Jen and Clive do not behave as if these onlookers are there.

CLIVE

After you.

JEN

Please. I insist.

CLIVE

I don't want you to feel . . . compelled in any way.

JEN

Of course. You want me to be here of my own free will.
You want me to want what you want. What would please
you most is to please me.

CLIVE

You're upset.

JEN

I'm not.

CLIVE

Good. Are you sure?

JEN

More or less.

CLIVE

That's a relief.

JEN

Why don't you ready yourself? I'll change.

Clive steps forward into the room. He looks around.

He pours himself a whisky.

Takes off his tie. Charles takes it for him.

Take off his jacket and shoes. Penny takes them for him.

Takes off his trousers. Monty takes them from him.

Takes off his shirt. The Housekeeper takes it from him.

Clive stands in his underwear only, sipping his drink.

*Jen re-enters in a negligee and high heels. This is obviously
highly erotic, but it must also be classy.*

She approaches Clive. The lights slowly dim.

There is a knock on the door. Lights up.

Enter two men in military costume and space helmets.

GUARD 1

Tickets, please.

The GUARDS each place a 'scanning gun' – something that looks like a miniature megaphone – next to everyone's head. Pressing the trigger emits a burst of red light and a vaguely futuristic 'beep'.

They check everyone. Clive is last.

There is no beep sound when Clive's head is scanned.

This one out.

CLIVE

What do you mean, out?

GUARD 2

No ticket, no stay.

CLIVE

That's absurd. I bought a ticket just earlier.

Guard 1 looks at the reading on his ray gun.

GUARD 1

It says here no ticket.

JEN

Oh, Clive, you promised you'd sort out the tickets.

CLIVE

How do you think *you* have tickets?

JEN

I'd *like* to buy the tickets. You won't let me. 'Leave it to me. I have a system.'

CLIVE

I do have a system!

JEN

And how's that going? You're hopeless!

CLIVE

I'm not hopeless. I'm just different.

CHARLES

Perhaps you forgot to buy a ticket for yourself. Easily done, old man.

CLIVE

With all due respect, Charles, that's entirely impossible.

JEN

Ha!

CLIVE

What's that meant to mean?!

JEN

Just that. Ha!

CLIVE

It so happens that I bought a family ticket.

GUARD I

Family ticket not valid.

CLIVE

I was *advised* to buy a family ticket at the kiosk.

GUARD 2

You got bad advice.

CHARLES

Is he to be held responsible for getting bad advice?

GUARD I

Yes. We hold him responsible.

JEN

You idiot. You're always trying to cut corners. Always trying to get the cheapest deal in town. Well, where's that led us? Where are we now?

CHARLES

Somewhere in the middle.

JEN

I do EVERYTHING. The only contribution you make to this family is buying the tickets, and you can't even do that. No wonder our children are so ill-disciplined.

CLIVE

Our children are highly disciplined.

JEN

Then why do they keep dying?

GUARD 1

Need children for family ticket.

CLIVE

When I bought the family ticket, we had children.

CHARLES

It's absolutely true. They had a lovely son.

GUARD 1

Then where children? Where is your son?

CLIVE

He ran away. I lost him. I wasn't watching.

Guard 1 takes out a gun.

Screams.

GUARD 2

Your choice. You leave or we shoot the old lady.

Guard 2 points the gun at Jen.

JEN

What the hell's wrong with you? He's in charge of the tickets.

CHARLES

Jesus, Clive. You're endangering all of us.

CLIVE

I bought a ticket!

How can you just stand there while they call me an old lady?

CLIVE

'Old' is your most obvious signifier.

JEN

(*to the guards*)

I'm sorry. My husband finds it very hard to admit to
making mistakes.

CLIVE

Stop undermining me in front of the armed guards.

JEN

They need to know the truth, Clive! They need to know
that they're dealing with a snake!

CLIVE

I am not a snake. And if I am, I'm a snake with a fully
valid family ticket.

He looks to the Guards.

Jen's upset.

JEN

Jen is not upset. Jen is sick of Clive and all that Clive is.

*Suddenly, Clive makes a run for it. The Guards catch him and
pick him up off the ground. Clive struggles.*

They throw Clive out of the house.

*The lights in the house go out, and Clive ends up in the same
wood in which we saw Jen.*

CLIVE

There is such a thing as blindness. You can't deny that. The
blind aren't refusing to see. They cannot see. And when
we are blind, if it is the case that we are in fact blind, we
cannot be expected to notice things that other people take
for granted. Things that may be apparent to you are not
apparent to me. We are dependent on others to see for

us. And to help us. To guide us when we are lost. We talk about empathy. But what about the non-empathetic? Who has empathy for them?

Jen walks up to Clive. She is now wearing a macintosh. He turns.

I thought I told you to wait in the jeep.

JEN

They took the jeep.

CLIVE

I wish they'd taken you instead.

JEN

I'm not who you think I am.

CLIVE

Who are you?

Penny enters from the back.

PENNY

Is this where you come to talk to the audience?

JEN

This is where we come to talk to ourselves.

PENNY

Do we need to go somewhere to do that?
                    (*beat*)
I'm the only person I *ever* talk to.
                    (*beat*)
Talking to ourselves is all we seem to do.

A *pause*.

Those were three options for my line.

CLIVE

I'm no acolyte.
          (*speaking to the wings*)
Does that connect? I don't know that the audience will remember.

249

PENNY

Charles and I had a daughter.

CLIVE

It doesn't follow.

PENNY

She was married. She was married to someone we liked
less than her. We lost her.

CLIVE

I like 'we lost her'.

Charles enters the woods.

CHARLES

We didn't lose her.

PENNY
(*rounding with fury*)
DON'T CONTRADICT ME. SHE DISAPPEARED! WE
NEVER FOUND HER! SHE IS LOST!

JEN

I could be your daughter. I am easy to find.

CLIVE

But you're married to me.

PENNY

Sometimes wives have mothers, Clive!

CLIVE

Not my wife. My wife's mother –

JEN

What? What happened to my mother?

Penny rushes to Jen. She takes her in her arms.

PENNY

My sweet child.

JEN

What happened to my mother?

CLIVE

                    PENNY
Mother's here, my dear. I've found you.

                    CLIVE
Your mother's dead.

                    CHARLES
Careful, Clive.

                    CLIVE
I don't need another father, Charles!
                    (to Jen)
Your mother was an accountant. Just like her mother. But
then came the Purge, and everyone in finance or legal or
paralegal work was wiped out. And then it was the retail
sector, and the healthcare providers, and the politicians,
and the teachers, and the factory workers, and the
scientists, and the shop owners, and chefs, and the people
in the service sector, until only the actors remained. And
then they killed the actors. One by one. Until the only
people left were in publishing.

                    JEN
THEN WHY ARE YOU STILL HERE?!

                    CLIVE
BECAUSE *I* WORK IN PUBLISHING. I SET UP A
COMPANY TO SELF-PUBLISH MY BOOK BECAUSE
NO ONE WOULD PUBLISH MY BOOK, WHICH
MEANS I'M A PUBLISHER. AND FOR TAX PURPOSES
YOU ARE CO-OWNER OF THE PUBLISHING
COMPANY, WHICH MEANS YOU'RE IN PUBLISHING
TOO!

He breaks down.

                    CHARLES
Come on, old man. There are worse things than being in
publishing.

                    CLIVE
LIKE WHAT?!

CHARLES

Well, you could be dead.

CLIVE

How do you know I'm not?

JEN

What about Monty? Why didn't they come for him?

CLIVE

He owns the audiobook rights for spin-off serials featuring his character from *StarQuest*.

CHARLES

That was a smooth move.

PENNY

I negotiated that.

CHARLES
(*to Penny*)

Shrewd and smooth. Like silk.

CLIVE

Which makes him a publisher too.

Enter Monty.

MONTY

I'm an actor.

JEN

Even though it's audio only?

CLIVE

It's a grey area, but yes.

MONTY

I need to act.

PENNY

We all have needs, Monty. We all need to act. We're all . . . dependent.

But on what? On what can we depend?

Tableau.

Curtain.

PART TWO: BEFORE THE PURGE

Monty is looking at us.

He sits on a piece of set that looks like the 'bridge' of a starship.

Behind him, a projection of stars.

My character, Co-Commodore T. K. Kwark, was one of
the most popular characters in *StarQuest*. Perhaps *the*
most popular. People related to his willingness to question
authority. Sometimes he's rash, but he has a good heart.

It's easier if you're not the lead. You can take more
risks as an actor. You get the B storyline, but often the
B storyline allows the writer's imagination to roam
more freely. Romantic intrigue with an alien life-form
might compromise the lead co-commodore's judgement.
Whereas I can be open to new experiences without overly
compromising overall mission objectives.

I like to take risks.

I can lick my wounds in sick bay.

Frances Munro once called me a 'moral dwarf'
and a 'shit actor'. I said, 'That's hardly fair. I'm a little
inconsistent, but I'm frequently believable.'

In one episode, Central Command orders us to revisit
Earth. There has been a Great Purge, in which the entire
population has been destroyed, apart from a small group
of people who still work in publishing and are ill equipped
to cope with a post-nuclear landscape. We are to retrieve

them or, at the very least, help them develop agriculture. The difficulty is in persuading them that the Earth needs more than a thriving book culture. It needs clean water.

Stirling – Stirling Munro – he created the show – Stirling wanted my character to fall in love with one of the publishers and stay behind to open an independent bookshop that could speak to post-apocalyptic discourse by foregrounding marginalised voices.

It was Frances who told Stirling that the fans wouldn't accept it. They would boycott the show. And, regardless, the Stardeck wouldn't be the same without me. I brought a sense of mischief that countermanded the show's tendency to over-literalise metaphors.

So I beamed back onto deck with the rest of the crew, while my Limited Imprint Lady Friend dissolved into tears, tears tinted vermilion by the chemical sky stretched above her broken heart.

It was one of our most critically acclaimed episodes. That was Frances. She protected Stirling. She protected the show. He depended on her.

We would argue over the scripts. I'd say, 'You can write whatever you want, Stirling, but I'm the one who has to sell it. There's only so many times I can ask for a full-spectrum analysis.'

Monty says the following as if they're suggested items for a shopping list.

Or 'I need an exact location fix,' or 'There's Cretian discharge in the transit shaft,' or 'Instrumentation indicates we've surpassed optimum escape velocity,' or 'Compensate the gravitational drift by neutralising the reactor,' or 'Calibrate safety circuits with the paranormic negative anti-gravs,' or 'Reverse the primaries' orbital drift via remote visualisation before we exceed twenty macro-spatials,' or 'The negative hyperspace-specific focus energy field is lodged in the transfer tube.'

Monty becomes more manic now, gesticulating and pacing around.

'Increase magnification,' 'Switch to auto repair,' 'Bypass the vision panel,' 'Lock in full auto,' 'Shift vibration files,' 'I thought maintenance had handled that . . .,' 'Ken! The command bracelet!', 'Search the fragments for traces of radiation,' 'Take a look at this – it's alive,' 'I can't override this thing,' 'Let us feast,' 'First you must rest,' 'It's this restraining field,' 'We've swept the complex,' 'I need an exact location fix' – 'Not an inexact one?' – 'No, an exact one,' 'As you wish,' 'As you command,' 'Copied, commander.'

When I came back from filming, late – no one works harder than actors – my son would be asleep. I had to walk into his room in the dark and let my eyes adjust so I could see him. I couldn't wake him. He needed his sleep. He had to sleep. I don't know what we thought would happen if he didn't sleep. It was as if his sleep was a precious, irreplaceable liquid we kept tightly cupped in our hands – no matter how hard we tried it would always leak out.

I would look at him, my son, face slack, drooling onto his blanket, his eyes angry and oscillating beneath his swollen lids. I couldn't be seen by him, because I had to go off to space. I had to go to another galaxy to take care of him. He depended on me. He was my boy.

Lights fade on Monty.

Lights fade up on Charles, in the kitchen. He talks to us.

CHARLES

As far as I'm concerned, the audience can fuck right off. They have no right to be there, and I owe them nothing. Nothing at all. I write for myself.

I have an audience because I am interesting. Because the audience wants to see what I have to say. And, finally, I have an audience because I can. And if I stop being interesting to them, I have absolutely no concerns about withdrawing. I'll go away. I will disappear. I have absolutely zero need for them. Zero. I'm doing this for myself.

I couldn't begin to tell you about the kind of shit I've been asked to write, but I won't do it. I'd rather starve. I've said to Penny, on *numerous* occasions, we don't *need* to eat every day. We've just got used to it. She said, 'We can't eat your pride.' Which is, of course, *exactly* what she'd like to do. Consume and subsume. But I like my pride. I'm *proud* of my pride. I don't want to cover my pride up with shame, like lime shovelled onto a corpse, so that it melts more quickly into the soil.

But since the Purge, I haven't been able to write. Or haven't *wanted* to. I don't know what to *say about it*. Or perhaps I don't know *whom* I would say what I have to say *to*. Because we all *know*. We all *saw* it. Perhaps I only wrote because I thought I knew something that others didn't know, and some kind of vanity in me compelled me to tell others, to elicit their approbation. But now I'm increasingly convinced – no, more than that, I'm in fact certain – that I know absolutely nothing.

Penny is in the woods.

PENNY

There are still people who can't believe that we – as they would put it – 'went along with it all'. Well, with all due respect, they weren't there. We did what we could. I mean, it was hard to know that what was happening *was* happening. I loathe the word 'normal' – sincerely loathe it – but that's what it was. It was all so bloody normal. And in terms of the people involved – by which I mean the people with whom I was in direct contact – it was really only Clive and Monty. And Monty I only knew through Charles. Through work, initially. Jen came with Clive, like a side dish that's been ordered for you. Every group has its limitations. I suppose ours was a certain insularity. A sense that we had constructed a citadel of sorts, and that it had to be defended. Charles was terribly private, in a way. He put on his bonhomie like a cloak to better conceal his hatreds. And I think he rather revelled in the oxymoron of being a reclusive extrovert. Well, now he has all the privacy he can stand. But the thing with a citadel is that once someone is in, they're in.

Clive was – and it's not a pleasant word – an acolyte. He was. Charles did not ask to be the object of his approbation, though he was susceptible to basking in praise's glow. Clive was just one of the many devotees for whom Charles would rustle up a 'casual supper', so casual that he kept little notebooks of ideas for them and spent days – I'm not exaggerating – days sourcing fresh fish and chard and various roots from scattered markets. Clive always lingered on, after the supper, to steal an extra few minutes with Charles. To grease the tin, to pour on a drop more of the old oil. He was, overall, a vastly unexciting presence, almost a pastiche of a person, and he never pretended to have even the slightest interest in me. But that all rather changed when he one day came along with Jen. Jen had been assigned to Clive as part of his work – if you can believe that.

CHARLES

I felt sorry for Clive. His was, from the beginning, a minor talent. One rooted in the parodic. His was a kind of fan fiction that sought to ape his latest literary idol, but it had the ghostly feel of anything that's uncentred. I mean, where exactly did he come from? I always ask people about their childhood. I will ask, for example, where they went to primary school, and – normally – they're off. It all comes out. That teacher hated me, or a promising career as a ballerina was cut short, et cetera, et cetera. But Clive – I think he said this, though I was so taken aback I didn't reply – Clive, when I asked him where he went to primary school, said, 'I don't know.'

I thought our paths had happened to cross, but it soon became clear that he had sought me out. It was no accident that he ended up at our table with his febrile wife. Who, by the way, was not happy. She was luminous, but miserable. Penny, over the course of who knows how many years, was unable to contain the rising well of her contempt, and it ended up spilling out. Not that I'd noticed. We were more or less separated, united only in our common love of the house we had. We had become two soloists by then. We played the same melody so often that it sounded like we were playing together, but it was only habit that kept us in tune.

Clive always knew the precise thing to say about my work. He would give the kind of compliment that wasn't obvious. That showed an appreciation consistent with multiple readings. God, it showed that he *was* a reader. And how many of those are left? We must read. We simply must. None of this would have happened if we lived in a world of readers. But we don't. We live in a world of watchers. A world of double-talkers. A sweat lodge of the misaligned.

JEN

Charles can talk. He can really talk. I've told him, 'You're not a writer. You merely take dictation from your ungoverned inner monologue. You're a dictator.' He laughed, but not for the right reasons. He laughs out a great hatred. It's a precious little hee-haw. There's nothing helpless about his laugh. It always looks as if he's trying to gobble up what you just said and absorb it into his own being. He swallows the absurdity and pats his full belly.

CHARLES

That we depend on each other is obvious. We know that. We are each wrapped in invisible wires of connection, and if you try to sever them, another tendril will have, unbeknownst to you, attached itself and gripped you tighter than before. So what I can't abide, what I in fact abhor is this attempt – and you can see it as the underlying bed of nearly every conversation – to get on top of someone else with words. That, I won't accept.

JEN

I wonder if anyone laughs for the right reason. If there's such a thing as a holy laugh. Not church laughter, not that feeble pantomime of self-deprecation, but the laughter of a saint. Not cackling, not sniggering, not the guffaw nor the soft hiss tremolo-ing through teeth. I can't imagine laughter without cruelty. What is laughter except for the explosive apprehension of failure?

CHARLES

People, then, would meet in kitchens. They would just sit around the table. You would cook and eat and talk and feed your animals and take phone calls and sometimes write, all around this same table, which became a kind of altar to multifunctionalism. It would be strewn with letters and bills and crumbs and bits of salt and rings left by water and wine. The other rooms were really just for the children. Or for storage. Or sleep. For when you couldn't stay awake any longer. That is how we lived. No one left the table.

The lights fade on Charles, sitting at the table.

In the half-light, he is joined by Penny.

PENNY

JEN!

CHARLES

Jen, don't you look marvellous?

Penny registers the compliment.

JEN

Ah, thank you – you're so kind.

PENNY

Don't be ridiculous. It's a pleasure.

CHARLES

Drink?

PENNY

Don't be a berk, Charles, she can't.

JEN

No. I can, actually. Just a little is good.

CHARLES

Good for you. Wine? Vodka? A brandy? Or a mix of all three?

JEN

Possibly just a small wine. A thimble.

CHARLES

I will put your thimble in a glass.

He starts to bustle about the kitchen.

JEN

Please sit. You must be tired.

CHARLES

Yes. Is it tiring? At the moment? It must be. Bloody hell. I mean, come on.

JEN

I'm fine. I'm just giving myself permission to rest.

PENNY

Charles never rests.

CHARLES

Come on. That's absolute guff.

PENNY

Which means I never rest. I can't. He's always bustling about.

Charles puts down drinks.

CHARLES

And how's Clive?

JEN

Clive is . . .

CHARLES

Clive?

PENNY

We love Clive.

CHARLES

Steady on.

JEN

And he loves you. Both.

PENNY

And when does he get back?

JEN

In just under a week.

PENNY

I remember when Charles was always off. He'd be dashing all over the shop, convincing himself he was terribly important. It was awful – I'd just sit here and cry.

CHARLES

Come off it – you were living it up. Off to parties, swanning about, chatting up blokes.

PENNY

I WAS HERE! I WAS ALWAYS HERE!

CHARLES

(*ignores Penny, calmly addresses Jen*)

And how are you?

JEN

Yes. Gosh. I'm so boring. I don't know what's happened, really. It's terrible. I couldn't say what I've done.

CHARLES

How do you feel about whelks?

JEN

Oh . . .

PENNY

You're doing whelks? She can't have whelks!

JEN

Can't I?

PENNY

Can you?

JEN

Oh. I'm not sure.

CHARLES

Not even a thimble?

PENNY

Shut up, will you? Why can't you do something normal? Who wants whelks or turnips? You've probably got a swan in the slow cooker. It's like living in a medieval settlement.

CHARLES

Whelks are predators.

PENNY

No wonder you like them.

CHARLES

What's that meant to mean?

PENNY

Birds of a feather.

CHARLES

And what's wrong with turnips?

PENNY

We'll find out one day.

JEN
(resetting)

And how are you both?

CHARLES

How would you say we are?

JEN

I'd say you are lovely.

PENNY

How sweet. We are surviving. Not much more than that.

CHARLES

Speak for yourself. I'm thriving.

PENNY

I sit here and try not to take my own life, but I have *no idea* what Charles does all day. He dashes off to that office of his and then creeps back here before supper, laden with produce . . .

CHARLES

How can you *creep* when you're *laden*?

PENNY

. . . puts on an act much like this one – and then fusses over these parsimonious suppers until I'm unconscious. He doesn't seem to sleep. WHY DON'T YOU SLEEP?

CHARLES

I SLEEP!

PENNY

YOU DON'T! YOU DON'T STOP! There's something FATALLY UNRESOLVED about you!
(*to Jen*)
I've never seen him sleep. I can't fight him. I'm exhausted.

CHARLES

I'm sure Jen didn't come here to see us howl at one another.

PENNY

WHAT MAKES YOU SO SURE ABOUT WHAT JEN WANTS?

JEN

I should go.

PENNY

You should stay. I should go. I'm very tired. I'm sure
Charles will make sure you get to where you need to go.

*Penny stands up and leaves. Jen starts to cry or, if the actress
isn't up to it, buries her head in her hands.*

CHARLES

Penny loves you very much. She's just in the middle of one
of her purges. Part of a wider campaign of reparations.
Have you taken yours with Clive?

JEN

Taken what?

CHARLES

Revenge.

JEN

What would I take revenge for?

CHARLES

Do you mean, 'What would be the impetus for your
revenge?' Or, 'Why take revenge at all?'

JEN

I'm not sure that's any of your business.

*Charles pulls up a chair and sits close to Jen at one end of the
kitchen table.*

Don't you think you should see how Penny is?

CHARLES

I know how Penny is. We've been married since before the
flood. I'd like to know how you are.

JEN

I don't think you care how I am. I think you just want to
kiss me.

CHARLES

I don't just want to kiss you.

JEN

You mistake vulgarity for honesty.

CHARLES

The truth is vulgar.

JEN

With what would you replace the truth?

CHARLES

Vulgarity.

JEN

But you just made an equivalence of truth and vulgarity.

CHARLES

I try to replace like for like.

JEN

But I don't like you.

CHARLES

I thought you loved me.

JEN

That's Clive. That's your wife.

CHARLES

And I'm not trying to replace you. I'm trying to kiss you, remember?

JEN

Check on Penny. Check if she's asleep.

CHARLES

Will you be here when I get back?

JEN

Where would I go?

Charles leans forward to kiss Jen. She turns her face away. He stops, pushes his chair back and leaves.

Beat.

Jen stands up, walks to the door and out into the woods.

There, as if waiting for her, is Penny.

Penny is smoking. She turns and looks at Jen.

During the following, at the back of the stage, a large 'Shape' begins to appear. This could be a globe or a rhomboid of some kind. But it must look like a non-organic object, and it must glow from within. This glow will increase in intensity as the dialogue continues.

JEN

The problem I have is that it always strikes me as overly convenient when what one might call the 'superstructure' intersects unduly with what one might call 'the microscopic elements'.

PENNY

I couldn't agree more.

JEN

So you could agree less?

PENNY

I could. I could agree less than I do.

JEN

But you don't.

PENNY

No. But that could change.

JEN

Of course. Nothing is set in stone. The last page of our lives has yet to be written.

PENNY

One hopes. Unless this is it.

JEN

Oh, yes. That would be dreadful. If this were the last moment.

PENNY

Oh, it'd be unbearable. If this were it.

JEN

What a waste.

PENNY

The waste is the most upsetting thing. The needlessness.

JEN

Probably best to say nothing at all than this.

PENNY

But what of those we'll leave behind?

JEN

What of them?

PENNY

I'm thinking of Clive, of course. And Charles, to a lesser extent.

JEN

Clive left me, he left me to die in the woods.

PENNY

Well, that's not strictly true. You left him.

JEN

I was forced out. I couldn't have stayed a moment longer. The situation was impossible.

PENNY

What situations aren't impossible?

JEN

Will you miss Charles, now that you've left him?

PENNY

I don't think so.

JEN

So you have left him?

PENNY

I don't know that you could ever leave Charles. What is it that you would be leaving?

JEN

Oh, I don't know.

PENNY

Did he try to kiss you?

JEN

He leaned in.

PENNY

How?

JEN

Like this.

Jen leans in, like Charles did. Penny turns her head away, like Jen did.

Lots of people say they like trains, but I feel they're like anything else really.

PENNY

What makes you think of trains?

The loud sound of a train going through a tunnel. It engulfs everything. Penny keeps speaking for quite some time.

When the noise subsides:

JEN

I'm sorry, I didn't quite catch that.

PENNY

I said, what makes you think of trains?

JEN

I suppose I always associate trains with Clive.

PENNY

He's a practical man, isn't he? And a very good driver,
from what I hear.

JEN

Yes.

(*beat*)

You couldn't accuse Clive of idealism.

PENNY

How long was that?

JEN

How long was what?

PENNY

How long was it before we started talking about men?

*By some contrivance, the object starts to move forwards, out
across the stage and, eventually, over the audience.*

Jen.

JEN

Yes, Penny?

PENNY

What would you say that was?

JEN

I'd say it was a shape of some kind.

Slow fade to curtain.

*Note: The Shape remains over the audience and slowly dims
down until the auditorium is dark.*

PART THREE: A SHAPE OF SOME KIND

Note: Penny, Charles, Clive, Jen, Monty et al. are no longer 'characters', but the actors playing those characters.

Our actors sit on chairs on a more or less bare stage. They have scripts in their hands and are now trying to 'block out' the scene. The kitchen table has become a rehearsal table – other bits of set may still be around, but they are 'set' rather than claiming to demarcate a room.

The Cook and the Housekeeper offer drinks, being now in the role of stagehands/helpers.

PENNY

I have to say that the only thing I miss is the scene where we had the lady on the table.

CHARLES

Steady on.

PENNY

The dead lady.
              (*to no one in particular*)
Is he going to be like this throughout?

MONTY

You mean the one my character shoots?

JEN

Or is it an accident . . .!

MONTY

Yes. Exactly. Very good. You see, I never understood why I would shoot her. I mean, is it that I mistook her for a marauder?

CHARLES

I don't read the scenes in which I fail to feature.

JEN

Is it meant to be that you still think you're in that show of yours?

MONTY

StarQuest? There was a wonderful exchange where I give my old helmet to my son, John Ray, but they cut it.

CHARLES

Child actors. Nightmare. That'll be why.

MONTY
(*quoting*)

'We could have used Kwantar's gills when they dropped the Big One, huh, Dad?' 'You bet, son. You bet.'

PENNY

This is why the author should be here. Otherwise we're making it up!

CHARLES

Well, we have the words. Our intentions must be buried within them.

PENNY

And we all know that words can only get you so far.

CHARLES

I think I met the author on a debauch. He was like an oak. He wouldn't bend. And he was gnarled.

JEN

Is he always like this?

PENNY

If by 'this' you mean 'inconsistent', then yes. Always!

CLIVE

I had one question.

PENNY

I'm going to take a wild guess: is it something to do with you?

CLIVE

Where do I go in the second act?

PENNY

There *is* no second act, darling. They're referred to in the text as 'parts'.

CLIVE

Well, whether they're parts or acts, I'm not in it.

CHARLES

Dear boy, as an actor, you should be thankful for any part.

CLIVE

But I disappear. I'm just not there.

JEN

But you're very present throughout.

CLIVE

I don't want to be a scent. I want to have some lines.

MONTY

I'm pretty absent myself.

CLIVE

You've got a massive speech! That long space thing.

MONTY

Just at the start – and then nothing. And, by the way, it's not really about space. It's about loss.

PENNY

What do you think space is? Space is absence.

CLIVE

Then I'm space.

PENNY

And yet you take up so much of it.

CLIVE

Oh, come on. That's below the belt.

PENNY

Yours or mine?

MONTY

I agree with Penny: we should have a director. This can't be done without a director.

CHARLES

In my time, there was the actor–manager.

PENNY

And had the Boer War finished by then or was it still raging on . . .?

CHARLES

You might, if I may say so, benefit from hearing about the theatrical tradition you are doing so much to undo.

JEN

Charles!

PENNY

Don't listen to that old ham. Even if he were crying over the death of a child, he couldn't resist putting some vibrato on it.

CHARLES
(*with vibrato*)

You lie, madam!

The Cook steps in with some sandwiches on a plate and offers them around.

Sorry, I can't have cheese.

CLIVE

I – and I'm speaking of the character, so don't *leap* on me – dominate the first act –

PENNY

Part –

CLIVE

Bit. Section. Movement. Chapter. *Part*. Whatever. And then
I disappear.

PENNY

IF IT WERE UP TO ME, WE'D ONLY PERFORM THE
SECOND PART!

CHARLES

What happened between you two? You used to be so
close . . .

PENNY

Well, Clive and I met, and then it went downhill from
there.

JEN

Isn't it obvious? They had an affair.

CLIVE

What we had was hardly an affair.

PENNY

It was certainly hardly fair.

CLIVE

Did you feel hard done by?

PENNY

I was hardly done at all.

MONTY

Why don't we put it on its feet?

CHARLES

Good idea. Let's put it on its feet.
(*he motions to the Cook and Housekeeper*)
Would you mind?

They take away the chairs.

Okay. Good. Why don't we start at the start?

PENNY

But isn't the start the end?

MONTY

Yes, isn't it all going backwards?

JEN

Honestly, I don't know where it's going.

CLIVE

I just want to know if it's worth staying for the curtain call. I mean, if I'm only in the first section, I'd rather leave during the interval.

MONTY

There is no interval.

CLIVE

I'm not surprised. This isn't a play, it's a hostage situation. It's a siege. We're all trapped by a misplaced faith in the redemptive capacity of art.

> (*beat*)

I'll go downstage, shall I?

> (*beat*)

What's the point. I mean, honestly?

The Shape dims up.

The actors can either 'find their places' and adopt a tableau, or they can continue, sotto voce, 'shaping' the scene between them.

Note: the voice of The Shape must not come from behind the proscenium arch but, preferably, from The Shape itself.

During what follows the actors lie down on the floor, one by one.

THE SHAPE

The play comes to me slowly. It overtakes me. It fills me up.

A pause.

At first there are no characters. There is certainly no set. It might only be a word. Or even part of a word, like 'th' or 'po'. Then I'll ask, 'Who said that? And why?'

A pause: four seconds.

Often I'll call the person who said that CHARACTER A. The person who asked why I'll call CHARACTER B. The names come later. The names I take from life. Everything I take from life.

A pause: three seconds.

Just as life has taken everything from me.

A pause: eight seconds.

There was once no play.

A pause: two seconds.

And before plays there was nothing.

A pause: director's discretion.

And before that . . . is a matter of debate. The word was the first thing, they say. Before thought, there was speech. Which explains a lot.

(*beat*)

Before speech, I try to think. But when I think, I use words. They float. They are in space.

A pause: nine seconds.

There is so much space. But there is only so much space for me.

A pause: twelve seconds.

Can I ask you?

(*beat*)

To make some space for me?

A pause: two seconds.

For me?

A pause: two seconds.

You can.

A pause: three seconds.

Depend.

A pause: four seconds.

On me.

A long pause.

                    CLIVE
                (from the floor)
I just don't feel I need to be here.

A long pause.

                  THE SHAPE
Your presence is vital. We depend on each other.

A pause.

                    CLIVE
Do we, though?

                  THE SHAPE
I depend . . . on you.

A pause: nine seconds.

                    CLIVE
I could be anyone.

                  THE SHAPE
I depend on you all.

Curtain.

New Views on Hughes
by Chloë Clifton-Wright

(Note: this article originally appeared in the literary quarterly *Promptings* in 2008.)

My parents were going through one of their periodic 'pinches' and insisted that if I were to continue to stay in their Marylebone pied-à-terre, I should at least contribute to its upkeep (this despite its near-inhabitability – no en suite to speak of, almost a mile to the Tube and a risible hob). Did they even know me? I wanted to write, not work. I was twenty-two and already exhausted. My father, himself a writer of some renown, though on the wane, was (I knew) unlikely to sympathise. He had laboured on a building site in his youth (something to do with stacking bricks – it took all day) and, during another dismal summer, had actually driven a van. And these weren't the proletarian affectations of my Cambridge (yes, Cambridge, I'm afraid, though I barely scraped a first) contemporaries, who fancied themselves as the next Jack Kerouac, cadging cigarettes and organising goat-herding sabbaticals in Slovenia; my father needed the money. His mother had been a seamstress and his father an alcoholic, almost by profession, for he was a landlord somewhere Up North and, if legend ran true, his own best customer. Before he came off the breast, my father was given whisky as a nightcap, which is why he finds it so hard to control his temper or come off the breast, especially those of his undergraduates.

'I hope you don't expect me to work in a bar,' I told him from a payphone (the one in the flat had been disconnected). 'If I want to be sexually harassed by a room full of creepy drunks, I'll sign up for one of your creative-writing seminars.'

'You couldn't afford it,' he snapped. 'And I don't do incest.' As if incest were the same thing as brunch. Though I suppose both, in their own way, demean those who partake.

I could hear my mother undermining him in the background. I'm convinced she has dementia, caused by the traumatic affront of my father's serial infidelities, though he insists her mental agitation has genetic roots, and that the anticipation of her decline was what drove him into the arms of so many others.

'Is that why you slept with the maid of honour?' I once asked my father. 'Because Mother contained multitudes?'

'Don't throw Whitman at me,' was all he could muster, before embarking on a ramshackle and ultimately unmemorable tirade about the primacy of desire.

Meanwhile, Mother is growing louder and demanding to know who would call at this ungodly hour of the afternoon.

'Who do *you* think is accusing of me incest?' I heard my father say.

'Could be anyone,' she replied.

And then they were off again, glibly silking their tangle-web of pitiful recrimination, performed as a post-liberal back-and-forth. Experience had taught me that I just had to shout over them.

'I will not work as a waitress! If you care so much about money, you shouldn't have had so many children. I refuse to scoop up slobbered-on plates. I'll die. It's a violation. It's like allowing people to spit on me. Which I'd frankly prefer. At least there would be an honesty to that. Why don't you get your faculty flunkies to spit in my mouth like I'm a whore?' I said, knowing I'd already gone too far but that I had to keep escalating to maintain tension. And, yes, I'm aware you're not meant to call whores 'whores' any more; you're meant to call them 'sex workers', even though the word 'whore' has more dignity to it than 'worker'.

'There's no need for you to be a whore,' Father said. So spectrum-y.

'Don't call your daughter a whore!' screamed my mother. Oh, my God, who are they?

'She's saying she wants to be a whore! I'm trying to dissuade her!' he screamed back.

'How have you allowed this?'

'I haven't allowed anything!'

'Why does she all of a sudden want to be a whore?'

'For the money!'

'What does she need money for?'

'To give to us!'

To be clear, and with regards to this whore/waitress axis, I have the greatest admiration for those who work in the service industry, but I can't rid myself of the thought that it's peopled by those who, for whatever reason, have given up on themselves. Of course, one needs financial resources, but with a little charm one is never far from a free futon and a small loan. Indeed, it's possible to shuffle between friends' flats for years. I have an older cousin who has never had a permanent residential address. Instead, he has a lock-up near the Elephant (how Hughesian!). He says it adds 'stakes' to the ordinarily staid business of seduction. If he doesn't get laid, he doesn't get to sleep that night. It does help that he's very attractive and speaks several languages. My mother's side are all linguists. My older cousin says the opening of the Channel Tunnel was a particular boon, as French women, though surprisingly less promiscuous than their British counterparts, insist on staying in good accommodation and get up early to go sightseeing all day, leaving one free to have the run of the hostel.

'Why doesn't she assist Harauld, then?' I heard my mother say. 'He's dripping with money.'

'I suppose she could assist Harauld,' my father said, as if assisting Harauld Hughes (1) represented a step down from bar work, and (2) was his idea. It turned out that Hughes's last assistant had left under a cloud. She claimed he had caused her to have a nervous breakdown, but Father thought the true cause was that she had an 'ill-formed animus'. And the more Father convinced himself assisting Hughes was his idea, the more he liked it. 'Could be a good way to see a world-class mind in the throes.' Hmm. I was always Team Anderssen.*

I brought up Hughes's spiky reputation, but father reassured me I was too much of a bitch to have a breakdown, and that if anyone were going to fall apart, it would be Harauld, because he

---

* Ibssen Anderssen, the Norwegian director of all of Hughes's finished films, from *The Swinging Models* to *The Glowing Wrong*.

hadn't had a good review in years. 'Besides,' Father explained, 'his other assistant was much less attractive than you. It probably got him down. There's something hugely dispiriting about employing a plain girl.'

Hughes lived in a nine-bed early-Victorian mansion in Holland Park. His wife, the theologian and chef Lady Virginia Lovilocke, still lives next door (though she has kept her main house in Chelsea). I got the Circle Line to Notting Hill and walked. I bought a packet of cigarettes because I thought it might help if I learned to smoke. A passer-by, a man, quite attractive but with too big teeth, helped me light the first one. I stood near a bus shelter, determined to appear normal. And though I didn't have a coughing fit like in the teen movies, I started to feel nauseous and had to vomit on the kerb. One of those small sicks that looks like glue. I left the pack on the bench and ran off. I knew Hughes hated lateness almost as much as the class system.

I rang the doorbell and, to check that I still existed, studied my reflection in the large picture window. I thought of Nabokov. My mustard flares appeared to be an acid green, and I had the sudden urge to run home and change into something that showed off my slim legs. I thought of a story told to me by an actress who is now a dame. Hughes once asked her if she would show him how she liked to be kissed. 'I don't know why exactly, but it felt like a perfectly reasonable question. So I showed him.' Afterwards, he simply said, 'Thank you.' I asked the dame whether Hughes was a good kisser. 'Not initially,' she said. 'But he was terribly keen to improve.'

A sturdy woman opened the door and ushered me into Hughes's study. Hughes lay on a chaise longue, his head laying in the crook of his right elbow. His left hand distractedly traced a figure on the floor. He was wearing silk pyjama bottoms and what may have been a judo top. I was later to discover that this, when teamed with white tennis shoes, was his rehearsal outfit. The sturdy woman asked if we would like something to drink. I asked for water. Hughes raised an eyebrow and turned to the sturdy woman. As if continuing a private joke, she replied, 'I'll see if we have any left.' Later, she returned with the slimmest water glass I'd ever seen; it was more like a test tube than a glass.

It stood next to two bottles of water, one still, the other lightly sparkling. Hughes had a Scotch in one of the biggest glasses I'd ever seen. It was more like a vase. It was 11 a.m. 'I shan't have another till just before lunch,' he said, noticing my noticing. He took a decent sip. 'I hear you are unwilling to work.'

I laughed. Or at least made the face.

'I thought writing was work.' I realised this represented a change from my previous position.

Hughes's face darkened.

'Gardening is work. Writing is a commission.'

I asked him who was the commissioner. He simply stared out of the window. Everything about the room felt expensive. He turned and fixed me with his black eyes and said, 'I can't pay you much.'

I started work the following week. Hughes was staging a revival of his very first play, *Platform*, his two-hander about a lonely Actress returning home from Up North and a vituperative musician (called simply 'Rocker' in the stage directions), a younger man who seems to have been sent to shake her out of her complacency. As I reread the work, I wondered whether the young man was Hughes himself. I put the question to him.

'He is who he is, just as I am who I am.'

So much for that.

The idea was to stage the piece in an actual railway station, at night. Where would people sit? I wondered. And what of the weather? And wasn't it a rather steep drop from the platform? At the play's close, the Actress jumps off the titular platform onto the tracks. On the stage, this can be controlled. Would it be quite so easy at Clapham Junction? Could this be the first theatrical production to be cancelled because of wet leaves?

Fortunately, we were, despite Hughes's noisy attempts to alter the railway schedules, unable to rehearse *in situ*, so we decamped to a draughty church hall in west London. It was my job to mark out the floor with tape, fetch Hughes his pre-lunch Scotch and make sure no one used his personal lavatory, which he called the Thunder Tunnel. Hughes drank a good deal of coffee, and one suspected that the lunchtime Scotch was, in part, to stop his heart from succumbing to some kind of caffeinated arrest.

This was Hughes's third time directing *Platform*. When it debuted in the 1960s, the director had been Leslie Francis, while the Actress had been Felicity Stoat. Stoat had since died and, what's more, had died estranged from Hughes. I wanted to ask him how he felt about it all, but Hughes did not seem to be a man given to talking, let alone to talking about how he felt. I tried to skirt around it. I asked him how it felt to see the Actress, first created by Stoat, being played by someone else. 'My dear,' he said, 'Felicity was a damn good actress. And I owe her much. However, she did not create the character. She interpreted the character. The character had already been created. You cannot resurrect the living!'

The new actress was an attractive Australian called Melissa, whose career was either just beginning or coming to an early end – it was hard to tell. The Rocker was an up-and-coming actor and musician who wore a poncho and eyeliner. After the first read-through, Hughes fixed him with his black eyes. 'Is that the volume at which you intend to speak?'

Casting this up-and-coming actor and musician meant the performance was already an Event. He lit a cigarette. 'I guess we'll find out.'

Hughes smiled. 'Let's find out now.'

A stand-off. It held for a moment, but then the boy from the local pub knocked on the door. He had Hughes's Scotch ready. The ice was melting.

A few moments later, I heard Hughes barking down the phone. 'You promised me he could act. He can't even speak.' I heard him not because I was next to him; I was actually outside, about fifty metres away, having a cigarette with the up-and-coming-actor-and-musician. I asked the up-and-coming-actor-and-musician whether he had a preferred brand of eyeliner. He said his girlfriend usually did it for him.

The next day, the play was cancelled. We were waiting for the up-and-coming actor and musician in the church hall when the phone rang. Hughes received the news in silence, before destroying the handset.

'I must leave immediately. I don't care where. You will accompany me.'

Hughes told his driver to take us to my flat. I asked Hughes why he liked badminton. He said he liked all games. Badminton was just the one he could play the best.

'Is playwriting the thing you can do the best?'

'What do you think?'

'I also like your poetry.'

'Thank you.'

He held out his hand for me to hold. I found myself putting my hand in his.

'A play is just that – a *jeu*, a game.'

'Is that why your work so often features games?'

'Let us do our best to resist banality.'

He let go of my hand. I hadn't particularly wanted him to hold it, but now I felt bereft.

'A game must have rules. Or it isn't a game.'

'And if it doesn't?'

'What the hell do you mean?'

'A game without rules, what would you call that?'

'Call it whatever you want. But it's not a game. It's a free-for-all.'

'But I don't understand why that can't still be a game. Isn't there such a thing as free play? Don't children just play games in quite an unregulated way?'

'Do you have children?'

I blushed. The question had brought the whiff of sex into the car. I opened the window.

'Have you ever looked after children while they're playing?'

Children appal me, with their crusty animal-themed blankets and overly bright clothes.

'If you have, you'll know the true meaning of boredom. It's endless, meaningless, a mess.'

I wondered what it must have been like to have had Hughes as a father. My own was largely absent. I suppose it must be hard to ensure your children safely participate in a variety of Improving Activities when you're scanning the incoming student body for fresh quarry. Hughes himself has hardly been a flag-bearer for fidelity. I asked if he had any regrets.

'You mean, other than agreeing to have you as an assistant?'

I must have looked wounded because I saw him smile. Perhaps sensing that this cut had gone too deep, he made an unbidden admission.

'I wrote a film once.'

Was this a Rosebud moment or the most boring sentence I'd ever heard?

'It was my understanding that you'd written many films.'

'You must learn not to interrupt. It's terribly important. It'll help you become less tiresome.'

He paused again.

'It was an original . . .'

I knew what it was. Once, as an exploitation-movie-obsessed fifteen-year-old, I'd attempted to interview Mickie Perch about it.

'It could have been . . .'

He tailed off.

'It could have been . . .?' I prompted.

But perhaps that's as good a thing to say about the uncompleted work of any writer as there is. It could have been.

The car pulled over. We were by my parents' flat. The flat I had helped pay for.

'Here we are,' he said.

And we were.

He offered me his hand once more, this time to shake.

'I'll remember you.'

'And I you.'

'I think my task is greater. You're much easier to forget.'

I watched his car drive away and, in a small tribute to *Platform*, jumped off the kerb onto the street below.

III

POETRY

(Note: the following poems and lyrics are taken from the
collection *The Wound, the Woods, the Well: The Collected Poems
of Harauld Hughes 1957–1977*, published by Faber & Faber.)

BUNDLE

The boy turned
And saw them
In the air,
Faces stretched with
An expanse of joy.
No reason
(Or perhaps
He forgot his offence).
Never mind, he was
Underneath them now,
With wind knocked out
And tears down his nose.
How long has it been
Since they cleaned this
Carpet?

EROSION

It turned to silt
And washed away.
It turned to shit
And stuck.

It fell to pieces
You couldn't flush.
The stink, the rot, it
Won't come out.

Did you keep a record
Of what you lost?
When you wake up
What will you miss?

Have you broken down?
(I have broken down.)
Where did the event take place?
(It took place near my home.)
How far from your home were you when the event took place?
(I don't know how to get to my home.)
Was the breakdown sudden, or were there warnings?
(No one warned me.)
Are you with anyone or are you on your own?
(I am on my own.)
Was anyone else involved?
(No one else is involved.)
Would you like to stay where you are until we arrive?
(I would like to be home.)
We are quite busy, are you okay to wait?
(I have time, but I'm not okay.)
Are you insured?
(I am not insured.)
And what kind of car is your car?
(I am not in a car.)
Perhaps it's better to stay in the car?
(I do not have a car.)
You do realise this is the AA?
(I know who you are.)
We help people who have broken down.
(I have broken down.)
People who have broken down in their cars?
(And what about those who haven't?)

IT IS SAID

He said,
What?
She said,
Perhaps yes.
It was. I mean, who
Can speak
For us?
Who, still, has a
Tongue since
They ripped them
From our mouths?
I think, he continued,
That, maybe, I'm not quite
Following. Did? As in,
Did someone take our
Tongues? Because . . .
I think mine is still in
My mouth. I feel it
Pressing against my cheek.
If anything, there's too much of it.
Shut up, she said,
The blood dripping
Through her teeth.

THE WELL

There it is.
(How deep is it?)
I think it still works.
(Is it safe? It doesn't look safe.)
It came with the house.
(What's the relevance of that?)
It makes a lovely sound.
(Are you okay?)
I came here when my wife died.
(You don't look well.)
It's below the water table.
(If you'll pardon the pun.)
I'm going to lie here a while.
(I wouldn't do that.)
Why not? Why shouldn't I?
(You'll spoil your trousers.)
I need to dig down.

THE WOUND

How wide would
You say the wound
Is?
How red is the blood?
Has it started to
Darken?

Can the wound be
Touched?
How open is the wound?
Does it gape?

(I measure it now
With my tongue.
I taste the hurt
And swallow it.)

I would rather you didn't
Do that.
(With the tongue?)
Yes. Or any other part –

(Of my body?)

Yes.

(You must give it
Time.)

I do not have time.

(You must let it
Breathe.)

I cannot breathe.

(You must let the air
Get to it.)

There is no air.
There is no ground.
There is just the wound.
It will not close.
I won't allow it.

THEN WHAT

Lost in ink.
Blood in mouth.
The rug worn through.
You wonder.

THERE

There.
Mouths interlocked
With screaming teeth until
They turned and saw me.
There.
What are you doing here?
How long have you been?
There.
What business is this of yours?
But it was too late.
They had already broken
The fourth wall.
I taped over it with
Something starring
That actor we used to like.

WOODS

Leaves in clumps,
Inefficient piles
Turning to mulch
As I turned away.

A sodden mitten
Plumed a trunk
Too small to conceal him
As he took that shit.

He pulled his pants up,
And then his shorts,
The steam still rising
As he licked his lips.

With an arcing swing,
He kicked through gorse.
Thereafter I hated him
As a matter of course.

BEAU'S SONG

(The following song was first performed by
Davey Brady in 1967's *The Especially Wayward
Girl*. Lyrics by Harauld Hughes, music by
Donny Chapel.)

Please dry your pretty tears
(And do not feel no woe),
For I, despite your secret fears,
Am very much your Beau.

Your mother is no more:
By truck she was so slain.
Her body broke to itty bits;
They say she felt no pain.

But how could that be true?
A lorry hit her frame!
If an HGV ran into me,
I would be might'ly maimed . . .

But let's forget your ma
(For now she's in the ground);
They buried all the pieces
(At least the ones they found).

So dry your sexy tears
(And do not feel no woe),
For I (despite your secret fears)
Am very much your Beau.

CLIFF'S SONG

(The following was first performed by Arden
Hall in *The Especially Wayward Girl*. Lyrics
by Harauld Hughes, music by Donny Chapel.)

You are an angel
Sent down from above,
And I'm just a boy
In need of your love.
A dog needs its bone,
A cat needs its flap.
A bird needs its perch,
So perch on my lap.

BEAU AND ANGELA'S SONG

(The following was first performed by Davey Brady
and Selbie Berger in *The Especially Wayward Girl*.
Lyrics by Harauld Hughes, music by Donny Chapel.)

BEAU
Being a model is very hard.
You gots to pose most every day.
It don't matter if your eyes are charred,
They'll take your picture anyway.

You need beefy arms.
You need a beefy back.
You need beefy teeth.
You need a beefy rack.

You gots to walk real straight
And keep your head up high.
You needs to never faint.
You needs to never die.

Because if you die,
You don't get paid.
That's the very first thing
My agent said. So

When it comes to posin'
I won't ever quit.
Keep that jukebox pumpin'
While your camera clicks.

But I won't forget my baby;
She's a highly qualified lady.
(Still she's studying like crazy
So her understanding don't get hazy.)

ANGELA

Being at school is tricky too
(Especially if your headmistress
Hypnotises you).
I harvest blood all night
And I sleep all day,
So I miss a good deal of the syllabus
And I'm slipping behind.
Oh, won't you come and save me?
But please don't be disturbed
If I maybe try to kill you
(For I am a wayward girl).

(YOU MAKE MY) LOVE BEAT

(The following was first performed by Davey
Brady in 1968's *The Model and the Rocker*.)

I feel it in my arms,
From my fingers to my feet.
When you show me all your charms
You make my love beat.
You make my love beat, girl,
You gots me in a whirl.
You're like prime-cut loin
On a butcher's block.
Your excess meat
Makes a juicy stock.

I feel it in my arms,
From my fingers to my feet.
When you show me all your charms
You make my love beat.
You make my love beat, girl,
You gots me in a whirl.
You're a pleasant-lookin' pheasant
Hanging from a hook.
When I see them feathers flap
Gotta take another look
As to why you're on a hook.
Cos that ain't right.
No, not tonight.

(The lyrics on the following pages were originally written by Harauld Hughes for the film *O Bedlam! O Bedlam!* and set to music by Donny Chapel. They are reprinted here with the kind permission of Lady Virginia Lovilocke.)

O BEDLAM! O BEDLAM!

In Bedlam, O Bedlam,
Confusion's the law,
Those left got no right
To see what they saw.
While all round the basket
Bread's piled in a heap
To keep out the hungry,
It's stacked up real steep.

We've brainwashed the workers:
They think they're on top!
We're knee-deep in bodies
And they're starting to rot.
Our leaders are babies,
They crawl and they puke,
Their fat fingers proddin'
The button marked 'nuke'.

In Bedlam, O Bedlam,
We're drowning in flames.
Forget the whole picture:
There's others to frame.
We're building a tower:
It's made out of oil.
We'll surf straight to heaven
On the blood that we've boiled.

This blood is from children,
These bones are from man.

These cries are from woman,
The sound of Bedlam!
There's no use in fightin',
You can't beat them all.
There's no use in standin',
You're bound for a fall.

In Bedlam, O Bedlam,
This state of affairs,
This death-shadowed valley,
This vale of our tears,
I sit at my keyboard,
I drift out to sea.
This island is sinkin',
It don't bother me.

(WHY DON'T YOU) TAKE A WALK (WITH ME) IN OLD BEDLAM?

The Man points the finger,
He don't like the way we roll.
Don't tie us to no nine-to-five
Cos that'll wreck our souls.

Why won't you take a walk with me?
I know you'll understand.
Why don't you have a talk with me
When I'm down in Old Bedlam?

This world it seems so crazy,
Good sense has had its day.
Us kids we got so lonely
We don't know what to say.

Why won't you take a walk with me?
I know you'll understand.
Why don't you have a talk with me
When I'm down in Old Bedlam?

We've gone to rack and ruin,
Or maybe just to rot.
We're tired of fighting day and night
For somethin' that we're not.

Why won't you take a walk with me?
I know you'll understand.
Why don't you have a talk with me
When I'm down in Old Bedlam?

(WHY DON'T YOU) TAKE A WALK (WITH ME) IN OLD BEDLAM? (REPRISE)

Who knows what's in the burning skies?
It gets so hard to see
These spiders crawling on the earth
And then all over me.

Why won't you take a walk with me?
I know you'll understand.
Why don't you have a talk with me
When I'm down in Old Bedlam?

Heard half the world got eaten,
They say it's outta sight.
I wish I coulda seen it
And took another bite.

Why won't you take a walk with me?
I know you'll understand.
Why don't you have a talk with me
When I'm down in Old Bedlam?

But no one seems to trust us,
They don't like us or our youth.
There's a riot all around us
And they don't tell the truth.

Why won't you take a walk with me?
I know you'll understand.
Why don't you have a talk with me
When I'm down in Old Bedlam?

(THERE AIN'T NO) LEAVIN' BEDLAM

(There ain't no leavin' Bedlam)
There ain't no place to hide,
Cos everythin' that's happenin'
Is happenin' inside.

(There ain't no leavin' Bedlam)
It's a wakin' shakin' dream.
(Ain't no throat that's tougher than the knife)
Don't matter if you scream.

(There ain't no leavin' Bedlam)
So don't you turn your back.
The spiders' eyes are on you
When the mandibles attack.

(There ain't no leavin' Bedlam)
Cos Bedlam never dies
And everythin' that's happenin'
Is happenin' inside.

Afterword
by Lady Virginia Lovilocke

Although Harauld is no longer with us on this earthly plane, he continues to speak to us through his work. His words are still so thrillingly alive that even after rereading this – yes, short – volume for the umpteenth time, I still rather expect him to ask, in that unmistakeable soft bark of his, 'Well, what did you make of it all?'

To which I would answer (oh, would that I could answer!), once he had staunched my tears with his black tweed sleeve and offered me a cognac truffle, 'I think it's perfect.'

'Which part? The pieces, the plays or the poems?'

'All of it. It's all too perfect.'

To which he would reply, 'You're perfect. But maybe if I ever write again, I'll give you a run for your money.'

Harauld gave us all a run, but not for money. Nothing Harauld did made money.

He made us think, he made us sit up, he made us who we are.

He demanded we tell the truth; that we remain – even in death – alive.